Longman Handbooks for Language Teachers

Mary Underwood

Teaching Listening

Consultant editors
Joanne Kenworthy and Michael Rost

Longman

London and New York

Longman Group UK Limited,
Longman House, Burnt Mill, Harlow,
Essex CM20 2JE, England
and Associated Companies throughout the world.

Published in the United States of America
by Longman Inc., New York

© Mary Underwood 1989

First published 1989
Third impression 1993

BRITISH LIBRARY CATALOGUING IN PUBLICATION DATA
Underwood, Mary
    Teaching listening. – (Longman handbooks for language teachers).
    1. English language. Listening comprehension
    I. Title   II. Kenworthy, Joanne   III. Rost, Michael
    428.3'4

    ISBN 0-582-74619-1

LIBRARY OF CONGRESS CATALOGUING IN PUBLICATION DATA
Underwood, Mary.
    Teaching listening/Mary Underwood.
      p. cm. – (Longman handbooks for language teachers)
    Bibliography: p.
    Includes index.
    ISBN 0-582-74619-1
    1. English language – Study and teaching – Foreign speakers.
    2. English language – Spoken English. 3. Listening – Study and
    teaching. I. Title. II. Series.
    PE1128.A2U534 1989
    808.59'07 – dc19   88-25862
                                        CIP

Set in 10/12 Times

Printed in Hong Kong
LYP/03

Acknowledgements
We are grateful to the following for permission to reproduce copyright material:

Edward Arnold for extract & table from p23 *You're Welcome* by Shiona Harkness & Michael Wherly;
BBC World Service for an extract from pp35–7 BBC English *People Talking* by Roger Owen. Copyright
BBC 1976; Cambridge University Press for extracts and diagrams from *Cambridge English Course* by
Swan & Walter, *Task Listening* by Blundell & Stokes. *Meaning into Words* by Doff et. al. & *Study
English* by Lynch; Filmscan Lingual House for extracts from *PAIRallels* by M. Rost & J. Lance & extract &
diagrams from *Basics in Listening-Short Tasks for Listening* by Asano Uruno & Rost. © Filmscan Lingual
House 1985; Heinemann Educational Books for extracts from *Let's Listen* stage 2(1980) by J. McClintock
& B. Stern; Lateral Communications for extracts & diagram from *Strategies in Listening* (1986) by
Michael Rost. San Francisco: Lateral Communications. London & Tokyo: Filmscan/Lingual House;
Longman Group UK Ltd for extracts from *Discoveries* (1986) & *Studying Strategies* (1982) by Brian Abbs
& Ingrid Freebairn. © Abbs & Freebairn 1986, 1982, extracts & diagrams from *Count Me In* (1982) by
Steve Ellsworth & extract & diagram from *Panorama* (1982) by Ray Williams; Thomas Nelson & Sons Ltd
for extracts from *Making Sense* (1983) by Rosemary Aitken & *Options* (1985) by M. Hinton & R. Marsden;
Oxford University Press for Table from p68 *Quartet* Bk.2 (1983) by F. Grellet, A. Maley & W. Welsing;
Oxford University Press (Hong Kong) for extracts & diagrams from *Better Listening* 1(1984) & 2(1985) by
Mary Underwood. Copyright Mary Underwood 1984, 1985. & *New Access Listening* 4 (1984) by Howe &
McArthur. Copyright OUP H/K 1984; Prentice Hall Inc for extract & diagrams from p87 *Spectrum* 1 by
Diane Warshawsky & Donald R.H. Byrd. © 1982. Prentice Hall Inc. Englewood Cliffs, New Jersey.

Contents

Introduction   vi

PART 1   **1   The importance of listening**   **1**

    1.1 Mother-tongue listening   1
    1.2 What listening entails   2
    1.3 Learning to listen   4
    1.4 Listening situations and purposes   4
    Conclusion   7
    Discussion/Exercises/References   7

2   The features of spoken English   **9**

    2.1 The sounds   9
    2.2 The stress and intonation   10
    2.3 The organisation of speech   11
    2.4 The syntax and vocabulary of speech   12
    2.5 Pauses and 'fillers'   13
    2.6 Formal/informal language   14
    Conclusion   14
    Discussion/Exercises/References   15

3   Potential problems in learning to listen to English   **16**

    3.1 Lack of control over the speed at which speakers speak   16
    3.2 Not being able to get things repeated   17
    3.3 The listener's limited vocabulary   17
    3.4 Failure to recognise the 'signals'   18
    3.5 Problems of interpretation   19
    3.6 Inability to concentrate   19
    3.7 Established learning habits   19
    Conclusion   20
    Discussion/Exercises/References   20

4   The teacher's role   **21**

    4.1 The teacher's objectives   21
    4.2 The elements to include in a listening course   22

4.3 General planning considerations 23
4.4 Before the lesson 25
4.5 During the lesson 26
4.6 Conducting the lesson 28
Conclusion 28
Discussion/Exercises 29

PART 2

5 The pre-listening stage 30

5.1 Listeners' expectations 30
5.2 Types of pre-listening activity 31
5.3 Authentic activities 31
5.4 The need for clear instructions 32
5.5 Teacher's books as a source of ideas 33
5.6 Factors which affect the choice of pre-listening activities 33
5.7 Limiting pre-listening work 34
5.8 Ideas for pre-listening activities 34
5.9 Pre-listening as an integral part of listening work 43
5.10 How pre-listening features in integrated skills work 44
Discussion/Exercises/References 44

6 The while-listening stage 45

6.1 The purpose of while-listening activities 45
6.2 The nature of while-listening activities 46
6.3 Factors which affect the choice of while-listening activities 49
6.4 Ideas for while-listening activities 49
6.5 The importance of immediate feedback 73
6.6 Teacher talk 73
Discussion/Exercises/References 73

7 The post-listening stage 74

7.1 Definition and purpose of post-listening activities 74
7.2 The nature of post-listening work 78
7.3 Factors which affect the choice of post-listening activities 80
7.4 Ideas for post-listening activities 80
7.5 Post-listening integrated skills work and motivation 92
Discussion/Exercises/References 93

PART 3

8 Recorded material or 'live' presentation? 94

8.1 Sources of material 94
8.2 The advantages of using 'live' presentations 95
8.3 The advantages of using recorded material 95
8.4 The use of video in listening work 96
Conclusion 97
Discussion/Exercises 97

9 Authentic or non-authentic material? 98

9.1 Authentic speech – definitions 98
9.2 Non-authentic material 99

9.3 Features of non-authentic speech 99
9.4 Problems with non-authentic materials 99
9.5 Features of authentic speech 100
9.6 Merits of authentic speech 100
9.7 The crucial factor 100
9.8 Reluctance to use authentic material 100
Conclusion 101
Discussion/Exercises/References 101

10 Criteria for the selection of recorded material 102

10.1 Why criteria are useful 102
10.2 The criteria 102
Conclusion 107
Discussion/Exercises/References 108

How to succeed with listening work 111

Typology 112

Bibliography 115

Index 116

Author's acknowledgement

I would like to record my thanks to Joanne Kenworthy and Michael Rost for their constructive comments on the early drafts of the manuscript for this book, and to Damien Tunnacliffe and Louise Elkins of Longman for their support and care in its production. I am indebted too to friends and colleagues who have influenced my thinking over the years and thus, directly and indirectly, contributed to *Teaching Listening*. Finally, I wish to express my gratitude to John Underwood for his invaluable advice and practical help.

Introduction

In many countries where English is learned as a foreign language, those responsible for the curriculum and the examinations have, in recent years, introduced an element of listening into their programmes. Whilst it must be recognised that this has been an important driving force behind the development of listening work, there is no doubt that, over the same period, teachers themselves have come to appreciate the value of developing their students' listening skills, not merely so that they can pass examinations but also for more general use when they wish to use their English in the outside world.

Even people who have little prospect of travelling to English-speaking countries will find that there are many occasions on which they will want to use their listening skills. The increase in holiday travel, for example, brings English speakers to most parts of the world and increasing communication between countries through business links and telecommunications provides many potential contacts with English speakers. It is important to help our students develop the listening skills they may need for further study, work or leisure, so that they will not be among the many people who, having studied English for some years, find, to their amazement and horror, that they are unable to understand the utterances of native speakers of English. This book has been written to help you help your students help themselves, so that they will be able to listen to English with confidence in their ability to understand.

In language teaching, the phrase 'listening skills' is often used to mean 'listening and understanding skills' or 'listening comprehension skills'. And this is the sense in which 'listening skills' is used in this book, where 'listening' is taken as meaning trying to understand the oral messages people are conveying. It has become common practice to refer to the material listened to as a 'listening text', and this meaning of 'text' is used in the chapters that follow.

1

The importance of listening

Listening is the activity of paying attention to and trying to get meaning from something we hear. To listen successfully to spoken language, we need to be able to work out what speakers *mean* when they use particular words in particular ways on particular occasions, and not simply to understand the words themselves. A speaker saying 'You're late,' for example, may be wishing to convey any one of a range of meanings: simply stating the fact that you have arrived late, or complaining because he/she has had to wait, or expressing surprise because he/she did not expect you to arrive late. What the speaker means lies only partly in the words spoken, and you, as the listener, must recognise and interpret the other factors which are used to convey the message to you.

No one knows exactly how listening works or how people learn to listen and understand. It is a skill which seems to develop easily for mother-tongue listening, but requires considerable effort where listening in a foreign language is concerned.

1.1 Mother-tongue listening

It is taken for granted that people can listen in their mother tongue with little or no effort. Even when very young we are able to understand at least the gist of what is said to us. It is assumed that this ability is the result of a number of factors, including the large amount of language and the number of different speakers we are exposed to over the years, and our acquired knowledge of the context, the speakers, the topic and so on. Even so, we sometimes have problems when listening in our mother tongue. For some listeners, for example, particular accents make listening difficult. Someone from the south of England may have problems understanding a speaker from the north; a New Zealander may fail to follow the speech of an American. For others, various topics cause problems. A mathematician speaking on advanced algebra may not be readily understood by a non-specialist. Sometimes, the situation creates bad conditions for listening. For example, in a very noisy room it may be hard to follow what a quiet speaker is trying to convey. And at other times a speaker may just go on and on talking, or reading aloud, for such a long time that it is extremely difficult to go on concentrating and then we may simply *hear* what he/she says without attempting to *listen* and *understand*. But these relatively rare problems do not detract from the fact that we generally listen to and understand speech in our mother tongue with ease.

1.2
What listening entails

Although we may appear to be inactive while listening, we must actually engage in the activity of constructing a message in order to be described as a listener. Whilst *hearing* can be thought of as a *passive* condition, *listening* is always an *active* process.

1.2.1
The aural process

It is thought that there are three distinct stages in the aural reception of an utterance. At the first stage, the sounds go into a sensory store, often called the 'echoic' memory, and are organised into meaningful units, according to the knowledge of the language the listener already has. Unfortunately, the sounds remain in the echoic memory for a very short time (probably only about a second). The listener does not have very long in which to sort out what is heard and might, particularly if listening to a foreign language, make errors as he/she attempts to organise the stream of sounds into meaningful units. The listener might be further troubled by the arrival of new information in the echoic memory before he/she has had sufficient opportunity to deal with that already held.

The second stage is the processing of the information by the short-term memory. This again is a very brief stage amounting to no more than a few seconds. At this point, words or groups of words are checked and compared with information already held in the long-term memory and the meaning is extracted from them. Once the meaning has been grasped, the actual words are generally forgotten. Again, the speed of processing is important. If a second 'chunk' of information arrives in the short-term memory before the previous 'chunk' has been processed, then confusion ensues as the system gets overloaded. The new language learner may be unable to process the incoming stream fast enough and will fail to extract meaning from it. As the learner gets more used to listening, and has at the same time learned more of the language, he/she can process some often-heard chunks more or less automatically, thus leaving 'space' and energy to deal with the more difficult or less familiar input.

Once the listener has constructed a meaning from the utterance (which may or may not be the meaning that was intended by the speaker), he/she might transfer the information to the long-term memory for later use. It seems that generally a listener who wants to do this recodes the message and stores it in the long-term memory in a reduced form. The evidence for this is the fact that when recalling something from the long-term memory, people usually only remember the *gist* of what has been heard, rather than the exact words spoken.

1.2.2
The importance of context

Recent work on the process of listening suggests that this is not the whole explanation and that comprehension can only occur when the listener can

good if it's for real purposes + topic linked

place what he/she hears in a context, even if this context has to be provided by the listener him/herself. Brown and Yule[1] say that the listener has to place language in a 'context of situation' in order to work out what the speaker means. Native speakers, when listening, can call upon their accumulated knowledge of the culture and background of the speaker and the situation and will know from previous experience more or less what to expect. They know that different types of people (young/old, male/female, shy/outspoken) are likely to say different things and speak in different ways. They expect certain kinds of language to occur in particular situations (at the doctor's, in a classroom, at an airport, etc). They know the kinds of language which will probably be used in relation to certain topics (football, music, cars, etc). They are aware that the way people speak to each other is influenced by the relationships between them (parent to child and vice versa, boss to subordinate and vice versa, shop assistant to customer and vice versa). From lifelong experience, native speakers can put what they hear in context, even though they may sometimes need to make adjustments when speakers do not say what they expect them to say.

One important part of this overall situational context in which the listener places what he/she hears is, in Brown and Yule's terms, the 'co-text', which they define as 'whatever has already been said in a particular event'. It is by placing what follows in relation to what has already been said (either by the current speaker or by other speakers) that the listener establishes the speaker's meaning. For example, a listener is only likely to understand the speaker's intended meaning of 'All right then, I'll come back on Peter's motor bike,' if he/she has already heard another speaker say 'I'm not going to fetch you from the party tonight,' and knows that this is a conversation between a father who is tired of fetching his daughter home from parties and a daughter who knows that her father does not like her riding on motor bikes. With this knowledge, the listener is in a position to realise what is going on and to predict the kind of thing which might follow (e.g. 'You know I don't like you going on motor bikes. . .') and would be surprised if the father said something completely unrelated to the previous statements (e.g. 'Each of these flowers has five petals.')

Using this same ability, a listener can frequently predict what the completion of an individual utterance might be after hearing only part of it. Indeed, it sometimes happens that a listener 'takes over', as it were, a speaker's utterance and completes it even before the speaker has managed to get the words out. As listeners, we often predict what will follow and then try to 'match' what we actually hear with our prediction. Even if the 'match' is not perfect, we are generally at least in the right area and have no problem in understanding. For example, when somebody says 'The clouds are very black. It looks as if. . .', we might predict that 'it's going to rain' will be the end of the utterance, but would not be surprised if the speaker said something else along the same lines ('it's going to pour'/'it's going to thunder'/'there's going to be a storm').

Simon Garrod[2] states that this context 'has to be taken into account at all stages of comprehension'. This suggests that the act of comprehension requires listeners to place the words in context at the same time as they process the sounds.

If the listener knows what is being spoken about, and preferably what is going to be spoken about, and something about the speaker and the speaker's intentions, comprehension is much easier. When faced with spoken language for which he/she must provide a context (and perhaps extend this context or revise it as the speaker goes on speaking), the listener has a harder task. If in addition the language is a foreign one, the listener's problems are even more acute. He/she may not be able to provide a suitable context (because of lack of background knowledge, or lack of knowledge of the speaker or the speaker's intentions) and may then resort to trying to derive meaning from the individual syntactic and semantic components of the utterance and the manner in which it is spoken, without having anything to relate it to.

1.3 Learning to listen

Since students need to learn to use more than their knowledge of the structure of the language – its syntax, its phonology, etc – if they are to be able to listen successfully, they need to learn not only to fathom out what is meant by the words spoken, but also, and at the same time, to establish or elaborate the context to which it relates. They need to apply both their knowledge of what Widdowson calls 'language usage' (i.e. the language system) and their knowledge of what he refers to as 'language use' (i.e. the appropriate use of the language to communicate with other people).[3]

If our students do not learn to listen effectively, they will be unable to take part in oral communication. Merely to *hear* what a speaker says is insufficient for communication to occur. When nobody listens to a speaker or when a listener fails to understand the message, we say that communication has broken down. This does not mean that the message has not been *heard* – i.e. that the sounds have not been received. It means that the listener has either not been paying sufficient attention or, whilst paying attention and trying to grasp the message, has not managed to understand it.

By 'learning to listen', then, we mean that we want our students to attend to what they hear, to process it, to understand it, to interpret it, to evaluate it, to respond to it. We want them to become involved and active listeners.

1.4 Listening situations and purposes

Many learners of English will find themselves sooner or later in a variety of situations where they will need or want to listen to English being used in real life for a range of purposes. What these situations are will depend on where they are living, working, holidaying, etc. And the reasons for listening will be many and varied, depending on what they need and wish to do. According to Kathleen Galvin,[4] there are five main reasons for listening, and the reasons our students will have for listening will generally fall under one or other of these categories:

(a) to engage in social rituals
(b) to exchange information
(c) to exert control
(d) to share feelings
(e) to enjoy yourself

Most listening occurs in the course of conversation. Each participant in a conversation switches role and becomes alternately speaker and listener. The main aim of oral language teaching is generally to enable our students to participate fully and comfortably in conversations, both as speakers and as listeners. And because many conversations do not take place in ideal conditions with easily understood speakers, we will want our students to learn to listen effectively in situations which even native speakers sometimes find difficult. Only in this way will they become able to deal, for example, with business clients whose command of English is poor, with participating in meetings in acoustically difficult rooms, with intimate discussion in noisy commercial or industrial environments.

Other listening situations for which we should prepare our students include:

(a) *listening to live conversations in which one takes no part.* This is usually referred to as 'eavesdropping'. A person may find him/herself listening to a conversation because something in what is being said attracts his/her attention and makes him/her want to hear more. The listener may not be especially interested in the overall topic and may have no particular purpose for listening. On the other hand, somebody might quite deliberately try to listen to a conversation with the very definite purpose of finding out what is being said. In either case, the listener, who is probably unaware of the context and perhaps unfamiliar with the speakers, is often not in a position to intervene and has to sort out the message without being able to seek clarification or repetition of any of the points.

(b) *listening to announcements* (at airports, railway stations, etc) where the listener is interested almost exclusively in extracting and/or confirming the relevant information whilst more or less ignoring the rest of the utterance. In this situation, the listener might just keep the newly acquired information in mind, or might repeat it to a companion, or jot it down in order not to forget it – all with the intention of taking or not taking action relating to it later.

(c) *listening to the news, the weather forecast, etc* on the radio, where the objective is again to extract clearly stated information, but the purpose for listening may be different. In the case of the news, the listener who wants to know all the main items of news for that particular day will listen equally attentively to the whole bulletin, while the person who is only interested in one or two of the topics covered will pay little or no attention to the other items. In the latter case, the listener needs to be able to distinguish between the point(s) when it is necessary to listen attentively and those when it is 'safe' to ignore what is being said. This skill of knowing when to listen also applies when a listener turns on the weather forecast but is only interested in the information about a particular region or a specific time of the day. If he/she knows the order in which the news items or the weather forecast details are normally presented on the radio, then it is easier for the listener to recognise the signals and to judge when to pay attention. Otherwise, the listener has to depend on being able to 'tune in' rapidly on hearing relevant opening words.

(d) *watching the news, the weather forecast, etc* on television, where the visual support is a help to the viewer–listener, who either sees the speaker

5

and so gets help in understanding what is being said from such things as the facial expression, the direction of the eyes and the movement of the hands, or sees scenes which relate to the topic being spoken about and so gets help in contextualising the utterances.

(e) *listening to the radio for entertainment*, where the listener often has very limited knowledge of what is going to be said or who is going to make the utterances. This is probably one of the most difficult listening situations there is. The language student who can appreciate and enjoy entertainment programmes on the radio will certainly have reached a high level of listening skill.

(f) *watching television for entertainment*, which is, of course, much easier than simply listening to the radio. The paralinguistic signals given by the speaker (the nods, the hand movements, the smiles, the frowns) all assist the viewer, as do the pictures seen on the screen. In fact, it is quite possible to follow what is happening on some television programmes without hearing the sounds at all (e.g. on sports programmes). However, some amusing, or disastrous, misinterpretations can also occur!

(g) *watching a live performance of a play* (perhaps in a theatre or a school hall), where the objective is nearly always entertainment. The person watching the play is likely to be interested in the story and the characters and the interactions between them, and will follow the play as an 'eavesdropper', listening and watching but remaining an outsider. The importance of following every utterance varies from play to play, but the audience is helped if the actors deliver their lines clearly and the production is such that especially significant utterances are given prominence.

(h) *watching a film in a cinema*, where the viewer is again an outsider, but can see facial expressions, gestures, etc more clearly than in the theatre. Another advantage of film over live acting is that the sound can be produced at exactly the required level and so the listener does not generally have difficulty in actually hearing the words.

(i) *listening to records* (of songs, etc), where the sound of the music might interfere with the sounds of the words, but where the rhythm, and perhaps the rhyme of the lyrics, sometimes help the listener to predict what will come next. Most people listen to songs for pleasure rather than for any other purpose, although many young students of English enjoy writing the words down and then joining in with the singing.

(j) *following a lesson* (in a school where English is one of the languages of instruction, for example), where the listener may need to grasp concepts and to distinguish between main and subsidiary ideas. During lessons, listeners can be called upon to respond to what they hear in a number of ways. They may be required to answer questions, to write notes, to carry out practical tasks, to discuss the issues, and so on. Listening in the classroom is often (and should nearly always be) accompanied by and integrated with other activities designed to promote learning.

(k) *attending a lecture* (in a college where English is the medium of instruction, for example), where the objective is simply to listen and try to understand the content of the lecture, although on many occasions retention of that content is also required and so listeners take notes to which they can refer later. To take good notes, listeners need to be able to recognise the signals used by the speaker to indicate that he/she is making a particularly important point, moving on to another point, making a contrast, or expressing cause and effect.

(l) *listening on the telephone* (to take a message, or simply to hold a conversation), where the listener is unable to see the speaker and may, in addition, have problems in distinguishing the spoken sounds because of interference and distortion.

(m) *following instructions* (given, for example, by a sports coach), where visual support and the opportunity to respond immediately by carrying out a task often make following what is said much easier. Frequently, the listener can cause the instructions to be repeated or broken down into smaller segments, either by asking the speaker to say something again or, if following recorded instructions, by going through them over and over again. When this is not possible, as, for example, when listening to instructions given on a radio or television programme, the listener has to hope that the producers of the programme have built in a number of repetitions or provided some printed backup material (perhaps in a journal or newspaper, or in the form of leaflets/booklets which can be sent for).

(n) *listening to someone giving a public address* (a political leader, for example), where the listener is often as interested in the views and attitude of the speaker as in the actual topic being spoken about. The points the speaker makes are listened to in this situation, but the way in which they are presented and the tone of the delivery are also important.

It is worth establishing which of these listening situations are likely to feature largely in our students' lives and to bear this in mind when planning listening work. This does not, however, mean that practice of all the other listening situations should be neglected, as students will find a variety of listening activities more motivating, and much that can be learned from one situation is transferable to others.

Conclusion In this chapter, we have acknowledged the ease with which people listen to their mother tongue and have looked at what listening entails.

We have seen the need for students to learn more than just the structure of the language in order to become successful listeners and have identified a range of situations in which listening skills are needed to fulfil a variety of purposes.

Discussion

1 When you studied a foreign language, how was listening treated in the course?

2 What kind of speaker do you find difficult to listen to in your mother tongue?

3 Have there been any recent developments in the teaching of listening in your country? If so, why did they happen?

Exercises

1 Make a list of all the different people (both 'live' and on radio/television)

that you have listened to in the last twenty-four hours. Then decide what your purpose for listening to each one was.

2 Look at a coursebook you are using, or know of, and check what proportion of the work is devoted to listening. Are any of the situations described in this chapter included?

References

1 Brown, G and Yule, G 1983 *Teaching the Spoken Language*. Cambridge University Press

2 Garrod, S 1986 Language comprehension in context: a psychological perspective. *Applied Linguistics* **7**(3)

3 See Widdowson, H G 1978 *Teaching Language as Communication*. Oxford University Press

4 Galvin, K 1985 *Listening by Doing*. National Textbook Company, Lincolnwood, Illinois, USA

2

The features of spoken English

It is important for teachers to be aware of the special features of spoken English which make it different from the written language. This chapter identifies some of these features and suggests the effects they might have on students who are learning to listen. It includes sections on sounds, stress and intonation, the organisation of speech, syntax and vocabulary, pauses and 'fillers', and 'formal/informal' language. Later chapters discuss how you can help your students make use of these features to work out what speakers mean.

2.1
The sounds

In English, just as in other languages, there are sounds which are unknown or unusual for foreign listeners, and which they may therefore fail to distinguish from other similar sounds or even fail to hear at all.

Learners may have difficulty with the vowel sounds of English and need practice in distinguishing between them, e.g. 'sit/seat'; 'foot/food'. For some, the consonant clusters are worrying as some of the sounds seem to be lost, e.g. 'exactly', where the /t/ sound is rarely heard in native speaker speech. And for others, it may be impossible at first even to identify consonants which do not occur in their own language.

Fortunately, understanding spoken English does not often depend on being able to distinguish between words which sound almost the same, because the context nearly always makes it obvious which of two words is being spoken. The 'ship/sheep' distinction is the most frequently quoted example. When a speaker says 'I'm planning to travel by ship,' it is easy for the listener to realise that the speaker is not saying 'I'm planning to travel by sheep.' The listener knows what the speaker is wishing to convey, not so much because he/she can hear the distinction between 'ship' and 'sheep', but because of the context in which the potentially confusing word is being used.

As far as listening is concerned, the use of long periods spent trying to distinguish between minimal pairs (words which differ from each other in only one sound) is unlikely to lead to any significant improvement in students' ability to understand what speakers say. It is better to deal with any difficulties as they arise and to take the opportunity at that point to give explanations and provide a little practice. The post-listening stage (see Chapter 7) is often the time when discussion of matters such as these can best be dealt with.

Even for students who have learned a little English and can understand their teachers and course tapes, the difficulties of following spoken English outside the classroom remain. Their teachers and course tapes have probably presented them for the most part with carefully enunciated language spoken at a fairly slow, steady pace. Now, faced with talk among people they have not heard before, they find that sounds are distorted, or elided, or lost altogether, as the speakers concentrate on the message rather than on their diction. Those with little experience of listening, but who have had considerable experience of reading and writing, frequently fail to connect the sounds they hear with words they have seen and recognised in their printed form, and find the whole experience confusing and discouraging.

An example of this kind of failure to understand occurred when an Italian student who had studied English for some years in Italy moved to London and attended a college there. Almost every morning, the teacher said something at the beginning of the lesson. The student, perhaps because her social expectations led her to expect that the teacher, on arrival, would greet the class, took it to be a greeting of some sort, although she felt it was not said with particular enthusiasm. She searched her dictionary for the word, but failed to find it. After some weeks, she decided to ask the teacher what it was that he said each day. In fact, they discovered that he was simply starting the lesson by giving the plan for the hour, and he had a habit of starting this by saying 'First of all, . . .'. The student had heard something like /fɜ:stəvɔ:l/, and had not connected it with the words that followed.

If the teacher had been asked to repeat the phrase, he would, of course, have pronounced it more precisely and the student would probably then have been able to sort out the meaning. This example demonstrates the need for such students to learn what happens to sounds in continuous speech so that they can associate what they hear with the language they already know in its written form.

2.2
The stress and intonation[1]

The English language derives much of its rhythm from the use of stressed syllables. The purpose of stress is to highlight words which carry the main information the speaker wishes to convey, and changing the stress can alter the meaning of an utterance even where the words remain the same.

Consider the question 'What are you doing?' in the examples below.

1 (*said from the door, with John not in the speaker's sight*)
'Hi John! I'm home. Where are you? What are you DOing?'

2 (*said as approaching Jane, who is in sight and doing something extraordinary*)
'Jane, I've been looking for you. Oh, my goodness! What ARE you doing?'

3 (*a conversation between two bank clerks who are about to go on holiday*)

ALAN: 'What are you planning, Martin? Anywhere nice?'

MARTIN: 'We haven't decided yet. What about you? What are YOU doing?'

In (1), 'What are you doing?' is an open question, expecting a factual response about whatever activity John is engaged in. In (2) it is an exclamation of surprise or irritation on seeing Jane doing whatever she is doing; in (3) it is a question which Martin has asked to discover what Alan, as opposed to anyone else, is going to do.

Students have to be helped to get used to the fact that words spoken in continuous speech are often not given the same stress as they receive when they are said in isolation. The problem is that students have often learned the pronunciation of new words by hearing them clearly enunciated, one at a time, by the teacher. The kind of words which cause problems tend to be those which grammar demands but which do not generally carry the main meaning: auxiliary verbs, prepositions, pronouns, etc. In a question like 'What are you doing?', the word 'are' often disappears completely (unless it is an expression of surprise), leaving the listener actually hearing /wɔtəjəˈduːiŋ/, which is easily recognised by a native listener but can cause problems for a foreign learner.

It is a good idea to draw students' attention to the way in which speakers use stress to give some words more importance. The analysis of intonation is complex but picking out stressed words is a realistic and helpful exercise. For example, a teacher might ask 'How did the speaker make it clear that she wanted you, and nobody else, to do it?' and the students might reply 'She said "you" more strongly.'/'She put a stress on "you".'

Close examination of spoken language reveals that people normally speak in short 'bits', with pauses of varying lengths between them. Within each 'bit' of an utterance, the speaker stresses the main information-carrying syllables and the rest of the syllables are unstressed and spoken relatively rapidly, so that 'bits' which contain different numbers of words all take roughly the same amount of time to say, and even native listeners may not hear the unstressed syllables at all clearly. It is well worth explaining this to your students as they will then not feel that they are failing to hear what they assume native listeners hear, and will not be led to believe that comprehension is impossible because of this failure.

2.3
The organisation of speech

Speaking is a creative process. Speakers are almost always in the position of formulating what they are saying as they go along and adjusting what they are saying as a result of the behaviour of their listeners or as a result of added thoughts of their own. There is, therefore, no certain way of knowing how a speaker's speech will be organised.

There are, however, a number of characteristic features which seem to occur in normal speech and which can be used by listeners to sort out what the speaker means. It is almost certain, for example, that important words will be stressed. It is likely that when giving instructions a speaker will repeat the most important points ('Put it, er, in the, er, in the top drawer. . . . Yes, in the top drawer.'). It is probable that, in a friendly chat, a speaker will signal agreement with phrases/sounds like 'Yes, it is,' 'Yes, quite,' 'Mm,' 'Mhm,'

'Yes, I do,' and indicate disagreement with such expressions as 'Yes, but. . .', 'Well, er. . .', 'Er, I don't know,' rather than simply saying 'No.' In most speech, a change of topic is indicated by a change of tone, and speakers may use a significant pause to indicate the end of one point and the beginning of the next one. In a more formal situation (a public speech/a lecture), a speaker may use a movement of the hand or head to show a change from one idea to another.

It is perhaps unfortunate for the non-native listener that spoken discourse is frequently not well organised. Even people giving lectures, which they may have planned very carefully, often produce a less organised flow of speech than they intended to (see 2.6 below). And speakers taking part in everyday interactions have, of course, generally not prepared and have to 'think on their feet', planning the next part of their utterance as they are speaking their last thought, perhaps changing what they are about to say as a result of their listeners' reactions/responses or other, external, factors. This process causes speakers to hesitate, to go back to the beginning of an idea and start again, to repeat themselves, to contradict themselves, to produce ungrammatical utterances, to change their minds in mid-sentence and go off at tangents.

A really disorganised speaker is hard to follow even in one's mother tongue. For the foreign listener, it can be a nightmare. And even when listening to a well-organised speaker, the foreign listener has to concentrate carefully, otherwise no sooner has he/she 'latched on' to what is being said, than the speaker has lost him/her again. To cope with this, students must develop the skill of recognising 'markers' and concentrating on searching for the message, not giving up hope whenever there is a 'hiccough' in their reception of the flow of information.

**2.4
The syntax and vocabulary of speech**

In *Teaching the Spoken Language*, Brown and Yule[2] identify a number of differences between spoken discourse and written discourse which are important from the point of view of students learning to listen. What they found from analysing extracts of conversational English can be summarised as follows:

(a) most speakers of English produce spoken language which is syntactically very much simpler than written language. One thing they noticed is that speakers use few subordinate clauses. For example, a speaker might say 'The plant died. They've been away. Nobody watered it. They'd left it in the sun, you see.' In written language, all these 'bits' would probably be linked together to form a sentence made up of a main clause and subordinate clauses: 'The plant, which they'd left in the sun, died because nobody watered it while they were away.' Speakers tend to deliver each 'bit' separately, leaving the listener to make the connections between the 'bits'. When subordinate clauses are used, they are generally linked by simple conjunctions ('and'/'but'/'then', etc) and the relationships between them are shown more by the manner in which the speaker utters them (the pauses, the intonation, etc) than by the syntax.

(b) speakers often use incomplete sentences.

(c) the vocabulary of spoken discourse is usually 'much less specific' than that of written discourse, with speakers frequently using words like 'it'/'somebody'/'they'/'you' (meaning people in general)/'thing', which can only be understood by relating them to the immediate context in which they are used.

(d) interactive expressions like 'well'/'oh'/'uhuh' feature in spoken language.

(e) information is 'packed very much less densely' in spoken language than in written discourse.

These findings confirm the need to use 'natural' speech (whether 'live' or recorded) for listening practice, since written language read aloud does not generally present students with the characteristic features of speech and therefore does not prepare them for listening to spontaneously produced speech.

The list (a) to (e) above also provides pointers to what teachers might usefully convey to their students about the nature of the spoken language. Simply knowing that speakers may not complete their sentences and that they use few subordinate clauses can be helpful to the student who is learning to listen. Being aware of the importance of the manner in which things are said is useful too. And learning to recognise the most commonly used interactive expressions (such as 'well'/'uhuh'/'mhm') and their role in speech is also valuable. Many students find it both interesting and helpful to consider whether similar characteristics feature in their own languages and how this affects listening.

Again, knowing that non-specific vocabulary ('it'/'somebody'/'you') occurs very frequently in speech may be helpful to some students, but, as Brown and Yule suggest, it is likely that this non-specific language is quite hard for students to sort out until they know something of the context and background of the utterances they hear. It is not a matter of applying one's knowledge of grammar but of being able to interpret what speakers *mean* when they say particular things in particular contexts.

Listeners who struggle to understand every word using their knowledge of the structure of the language to decipher the message often have problems. They tend to get confused and will probably be less successful than listeners who seek the meaning without focussing overmuch on the language. In many instances, listeners do not have the time to unravel the mix of structures used by the speaker before they receive the next part of the message. But, more importantly, they are frequently in a position where simply using their knowledge of 'correct' grammar to sort out the message does not work.

**2.5
Pauses and
'fillers'**

The pauses which occur in speech give the listener time to think about what has just been said and to relate it to what has gone before. At the beginning of their courses, students will find it easier to listen to speakers who, whilst speaking at their normal speed (provided it is not particularly fast), make quite long pauses between the 'bits' of their utterances. The length of pause used will depend on the speaker's speech habits, on the behaviour and reactions of those listening (if the speaker can see them), and on the speaker's need to work out what to say next.

Long gaps in speech are often filled with sounds/expressions such as

'Er. . .'/'Erm. . .'/'and er. . .' simply to avoid long silences, which are generally thought to be rather embarrassing in English conversation. It is a good idea to explain the use of these 'fillers', particularly to speakers of languages in which long silences are a normal feature of conversation, so that they can recognise them and know that they are not part of the essential message.

2.6 Formal/informal language

A distinction is sometimes made between the language spoken in 'formal' situations and the language used in 'informal' situations as, for example, a lecture and a chat between friends.

A lecture or a public address is expected to consist of relatively well-organised speech, using more structured language than would be heard in informal conversation, because most lecturers and public speakers plan in advance what they intend to say, and may have notes, or even a complete text, to guide them through the speech. The language they use tends more towards written language than that used in ordinary everyday talk and is often described as 'formal' to contrast it with the 'informal' language of spontaneously produced speech.

Unfortunately for the language learner, the division is not as neat as this. It frequently happens, for example, that a lecturer delivering a very formal lecture from a prepared set of notes switches to informal language when making an aside or recounting an anecdote as an illustration of a point just made. Or a person involved in describing a complicated phenomenon to a friend over coffee may switch in and out of formal and informal styles depending on whether he/she is describing the phenomenon or commenting on it. A good example of this is a doctor talking to a friend about a medical condition which the friend is suffering from. The doctor will probably describe the condition in fairly formal language and then go on to explain it in more informal language, perhaps using even more informal language to give examples of the effect it has had on other people.

Between the extremes, there is a range of formality/informality, depending on the social setting, the relative ages and status of the speaker and listener, their attitudes to each other and the topic, the extent to which they share the same background knowledge, and so on.

Many language learners have limited experience of English language in informal situations. In their lessons they tend to use formal language, because this is what is expected when teachers and students talk to each other, and so they have difficulty in understanding informal spoken discourse. They have particular difficulty when switching to informal language when it occurs within what is otherwise a formal situation. For the foreign language listener, judging the importance of these interspersed informal utterances is a problem. Being able to establish the significance not only of *what* is said, but of *how* it is being said, is an important listening skill.

Conclusion

This chapter has highlighted the features which characterise spoken English which can, and must, be taken into account by listeners as they attempt to discover the real meaning of what they hear.

Discussion

1 How useful do you think it would be for *your* students to learn about the features of spoken English?
2 What sounds cause particular difficulties for your students in listening comprehension work? Why do you think this is so?

Exercises

1 Listen to a short recording of spontaneous speech in your native language and check to what extent it differs from the written language. You may need to listen a number of times to identify specific features.
2 Try holding a conversation with a friend using only complete sentences and not allowing any false starts. Then try the same exercise in another language. How does it feel? What do you notice?

References

1 Stress and intonation is a large and complex area which is dealt with more comprehensively in Kenworthy, J 1987 *Teaching English Pronunciation*. Longman
2 Brown, G and Yule, G 1983 *Teaching the Spoken Language*. Cambridge University Press

3

Potential problems in learning to listen to English

Language learners often feel inundated with problems when they first attempt to listen to a new language. Although the problems are many and various, they are not all experienced by all students, nor are they experienced to the same degree by students from different backgrounds. It is noticeable, for example, that students whose culture and education includes a strong storytelling and oral communication tradition are generally 'better' at listening than those from a reading and book-based culture and educational background. It also seems that students for whom the stress and intonation which occur in English are reasonably familiar have less trouble than those whose own language is based on different rhythms and tones.

Whatever the reasons for these problems, it is important to recognise the features of the spoken language and to understand how they affect language learners, so that they can be borne in mind when selecting and using listening materials and activities.

In Chapter 1 we looked in general at what listening entails. In this chapter, we focus more specifically on the learners and the problems that they may encounter when learning to listen.

3.1
Lack of control over the speed at which speakers speak

Many English language learners believe that the greatest difficulty with listening comprehension, as opposed to reading comprehension, is that the listener cannot control how quickly a speaker speaks. They feel that the utterances disappear, as it were, before they can sort them out, whereas the words in a written text remain on the page where the reader can glance back at them or re-examine them thoroughly. This frequently means that students who are learning to listen cannot keep up. They are so busy working out the meaning of one part of what they hear that they miss the next part. Or they simply ignore a whole chunk because they fail to sort it all out quickly enough. Either way, they fail.

3.2
Not being able to get things repeated

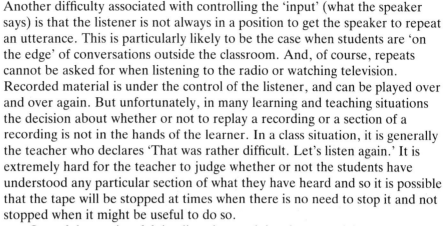

Another difficulty associated with controlling the 'input' (what the speaker says) is that the listener is not always in a position to get the speaker to repeat an utterance. This is particularly likely to be the case when students are 'on the edge' of conversations outside the classroom. And, of course, repeats cannot be asked for when listening to the radio or watching television. Recorded material is under the control of the listener, and can be played over and over again. But unfortunately, in many learning and teaching situations the decision about whether or not to replay a recording or a section of a recording is not in the hands of the learner. In a class situation, it is generally the teacher who declares 'That was rather difficult. Let's listen again.' It is extremely hard for the teacher to judge whether or not the students have understood any particular section of what they have heard and so it is possible that the tape will be stopped at times when there is no need to stop it and not stopped when it might be useful to do so.

One of the merits of doing listening work in a language laboratory, or listening centre, is that the students can be given the opportunity to control their own machines and proceed in whatever way they wish, going back over parts they want to hear again as often as they feel necessary, or pressing on and forcing themselves to listen at the speed of the recording.

3.3
The listener's limited vocabulary

Choice of vocabulary is in the hands of the speaker, not the listener. The listener has to do the best he/she can to follow, although in some circumstances it is possible to stop the speaker and ask for clarification. Sometimes, listeners can deduce the meaning of a word from its context. This is something that frequently occurs in mother-tongue listening when a word is not understood or not heard clearly. For people listening to a foreign language, an unknown word can be like a suddenly dropped barrier causing them to stop and think about the meaning of the word and thus making them miss the next part of the speech. It is believed that this tendency to stop listening and concentrate on the immediate problem often results when learners have been taught their English in a way which has given more emphasis to accuracy than fluency and which has been more concerned with mastery of the forms of language rather than with how it is used. This style of teaching leads students to focus on the language word by word, to work out its structure, and then to decide on its meaning. In listening, this method does not work. It really is a case of 'He who hesitates is lost'!

Indeed, determination to listen to what is coming, and letting things that have passed go rather than dwelling upon them, often gives surprisingly good results. Speakers often say things more than once, or rephrase them, or another speaker echoes what has been said. The listener who has not 'stopped' to dwell on a half-missed point gets a second, or even third chance to fill the gap in the message he/she is receiving.

The following transcript of part of a conversation about dogs illustrates this point:

STEPHENS: Uhm. Sometimes it's difficult dealing with . . . with some people, but . . . I – I think . . . I think it's nice that people love their pets too.

INTERVIEWER: But I've heard it said uh. . .

STEPHENS: The – It's funny when you . . . when you get into some fanatics, I have to admit. There was one lady that . . . bought a coffin for her dog, and for six months she . . .

INTERVIEWER: A coffin . . ?

STEPHENS: A coffin for her dog – it was a thousand-dollar coffin. And then for six months, she slept on the floor with the dog. The dog was ha – was in heart failure. And she – every . . . every – you know, the dog could't go anywhere, so she just stayed with the dog all the time. And finally, she decided it was time for the dog to . . . to die, and so they had a little ser – uhm . . . service for it before the doctor – The doctor had to go out to the house and euthanize the dog. They had a little service first, and then they talked about the dog, and what a nice dog it had been. And then he euthanized the dog. And then they put it in the coffin, and then they buried it out in the backyard.

INTERVIEWER: . . . it was a thousand dollars?

STEPHENS: Uh-hmm. There's things like that you hear. I mean, I – There's – There are a few things like that where people are really fanatics.

From Edwin T Cornelius Jr *Interview*, page 139, Longman, New York. 1981

Students need to develop the skill of keeping up with the speaker (even being ahead of the speaker) even if this means letting parts which they have failed to sort out pass. Professor H H Stern says that the good language learner is the one who 'can tolerate vagueness and incompleteness of knowledge'.[1] This is especially true of good listeners.

There is no doubt that in our own native language we frequently understand only a part of what a speaker means but we are generally able to continue with the interaction and to respond. It is what Brown and Yule[2] call 'this expectation, this habit, of *tolerable* mutual comprehension which we wish our students to achieve, not the total comprehension of everything said and meant, which is completely beyond the powers of native listeners.'

3.4 Failure to recognise the 'signals'

There are many ways in which a speaker can indicate that he/she is moving from one point to another, or giving an example, or repeating a point, or whatever. These signals are not immediately self-evident to a person listening to a foreign language and can easily be missed.

Lecturers, for example, in a formal situation (see 2.6) generally show clearly that they are about to begin a new point. They use expressions like 'Secondly, . . .' or 'Then, . . .'. They may pause or make a gesture or move slightly. They may mark a change to a new point by increased loudness or a clear change of pitch. In spontaneous conversation, a speaker will make use of different intonation to indicate whether he/she is introducing a new idea or saying something the listener already knows.

Students need to learn to listen (and, if the speaker is visible, watch) for the 'signals' in order to be able to connect the various utterances in the way the speaker intended them to be connected.

**3.5
Problems of
interpretation**

Sharing common meanings and assumptions makes communication possible. Students who are unfamiliar with the context may have considerable difficulty in *interpreting* the words they hear even if they can understand their 'surface' meaning. 'The snow's very bad so there's nobody in the office' might be difficult for students who have never experienced snow to interpret correctly. And the meaning of non-verbal clues – facial expression, nods, gestures, tone of voice – can easily be misinterpreted by listeners from other cultures.

Problems of interpretation can even occur when the speaker and the listener are from the same background and use the same language. For example, if you have an appointment with somebody you do not know and then that person phones you and says 'I'll be a bit late,' you will not know what 'a bit' means, but if an old friend with whom you have an appointment phones and says the same thing, you will probably know how long you will have to wait because the friend in question is always about half an hour late.

**3.6
Inability to
concentrate**

Inability to concentrate can be caused by a number of things, but in listening work it is a major problem, because even the shortest break in attention can seriously impair comprehension. If students find the topic interesting, they will find concentration easier. But sometimes, even when the topic is interesting, students simply find listening work very tiring, because they make an enormous effort (often greater than is useful) to follow what they hear word by word.

Outside factors may well make concentration difficult, too. If recorded material is being used, an inferior machine or poor recording can make it very hard for the students. Some rooms are acoustically unsuitable for the use of recorded materials. But the desirability of providing students with the great variety of voices and topics which recorded materials can bring to the classroom make it well worth struggling to provide these opportunities.

**3.7
Established
learning habits**

Traditionally, teachers have aimed to teach their students to understand everything in the English lesson, and have gone to considerable trouble to ensure that they do, by repeating and pronouncing words carefully, by grading the language to suit their level, by speaking slowly and pausing frequently. Because of this, students are worried if they fail to understand a particular word or phrase when they are listening, and become discouraged by their lack of success. This is a particularly difficult problem for those teachers who have themselves learned English mainly through reading and writing and who, therefore, find it as hard to 'tolerate vagueness and incompleteness of knowledge' (Stern[1]) as their students do. But it is only by overcoming these worries and encouraging students to 'take chances' as they seek to understand that we shall be able to prepare them for the listening experiences they will have outside the classroom. David Forman[3] talks about students who are unprepared for 'the problems of comprehending a native speaker who makes no concessions to their status as a learner' and says that 'When the learner can more readily accept the frustrations involved, he will be more prepared to strive for a partial and incomplete understanding of what is being said.'

Conclusion

In this chapter, we have examined some of the major problems which may be encountered in learning to listen. We have considered the students' lack of control over what the speaker says and how he/she says it, the students' lack of vocabulary and their possible failure to recognise the 'signals', as well as their inability to concentrate and their past learning habits.

Discussion

1 Which of the problems mentioned in this chapter do you think is the most difficult to overcome for your students?
2 Consider whether your own study of a foreign language encouraged you to 'tolerate vagueness and incompleteness of knowledge'. How far do you think this ability is useful in language learning?

Exercises

1 Think of at least three meanings which each of the following might have depending on its context, the manner in which it is spoken, etc:

(a) What time will you be home?
(b) It's hot in here.
(c) Have you been to the new Chinese restaurant?

2 Listen to a recording in a foreign language you have learned (preferably just a little) and consider what problems you have as you listen. Are they the same as the ones discussed in this chapter?

References

1 Stern, H H 1975 What can we learn from the good language learner? *Canadian Modern Language Review* **31**
2 Brown, G and Yule, G 1983 *Teaching the Spoken Language*. Cambridge University Press
3 Forman, D 1986 *Factors affecting the choice of relevant listening material for Malaysian students planning to study at English medium institutes of higher education overseas*. University of Wales Institute of Science and Technology, Cardiff (unpublished)

4

The teacher's role

4.1
The teacher's objectives

One of the main arguments used to justify the *exclusion* of listening from the curriculum in the past was that listening cannot be taught. It was claimed that people could only be offered practice which might help them apply their already developed listening skills to the language being learned. This justification is unacceptable if we believe that 'to teach' means 'to facilitate learning' and if we see the role of the teacher as being the support and guidance of learners. Students will naturally turn to their teachers when they find they are having difficulty in understanding spoken English and teachers will wish to assist in whatever ways they can.

Whilst it is not known precisely what occurs inside a listener's head during the process of listening it *is* possible to provide opportunities for students to consider the problems they encounter and to support them in their attempts so that they are likely to become better at listening.

The teacher's objectives should include:

(a) *exposing students to a range of listening experiences*

This can be done by using a lot of different listening texts (stories, conversations, descriptive talks, etc) which incorporate a variety of language (formal or informal, spoken by native speakers or foreign speakers, delivered slowly or quickly).

(b) *making listening purposeful for the students*

This can best be achieved by providing tasks which are as realistic as possible, so that the students can relate what they are doing in the lesson to things that happen in real life, outside the classroom.

(c) *helping students understand what listening entails and how they might approach it*

Often, this means changing the attitudes of students, particularly if in the past their attempts to learn to listen have been unsuccessful. It is worth spending a little time explaining the processes of listening to your students (in their own language if necessary) and talking to them about how they listen in their native language.

(d) *building up students' confidence in their own listening ability*

Success breeds success, and students who feel they are succeeding will be encouraged to go on trying. The teacher's role in this is to provide experiences and activities in which students can be successful. It is important to remove the idea of 'testing' from listening activities and to take advantage of the almost universal interest in problem-solving as a basis for most of your listening work.

4.2 The elements to include in a listening course

Students will become more proficient in listening to English if (a) they apply the strategies they use naturally in mother-tongue listening rather than getting 'bogged down' and discouraged by trying to follow the spoken language word by word; (b) they increase their knowledge of the cultural context in which the language is being spoken; and (c) they accept that partial interpretation of what they hear is often sufficient for understanding.

Teachers therefore need to provide planned and systematic opportunities for their students to learn how to:

– determine what an utterance or a conversation is about (even if they cannot follow the details);
– establish who is talking and to whom (e.g. a doctor talking to a patient);
– recognise the mood and attitude of the speaker(s) (e.g. an angry parent, a persuasive salesperson).

If in addition the listener is overhearing the conversation (e.g. on the radio) rather than participating in it, students need to be able to:

– decide *where* a conversation is taking place (e.g. in a hospital, on a bus);
– decide *when* a conversation is taking place (e.g. after a football match, before a business meeting).

For each of the above, students' awareness of what signals they have used to reach their decisions needs to be heightened, so that they will be able to use them more easily in future. They will, for example, need to learn:

– to be aware of how lexis and lexical sets can indicate topic;
– to interpret the use of stress, intonation, loudness, etc;
– to recognise transition words and what they indicate (e.g. 'although', 'for instance', 'but', 'for example');
– to predict what is coming next in an utterance or a conversation, using both their general knowledge and the clues from what they have heard;
– to make guesses based on the context, the tone, etc;
– to 'listen between the words' (the listening equivalent to 'reading between the lines') to know what is *really* meant by speakers who do not always say precisely what they mean;
– to distinguish between facts and opinions as they listen, so that they can be critical listeners, not easily persuaded by other people's clever use of

language (e.g. utterances where 'spying on' is used rather than 'watching', to suggest that there was something suspicious/sinister about the action).

And, to take part successfully in conversations, the students also need to have practice in turn-taking (being alternately speaker and listener), and in giving feedback to the speaker (e.g. by nodding, saying 'Uh uh' or 'Mmm').

Whilst using a wide selection of listening text types and asking your students to carry out a range of activities (see Chapters 5, 6 and 7), you should try to ensure that the focus of each lesson is on one or two of the strategies that need to be exercised so that your students come to understand how those particular strategies can assist them in developing their overall listening skills.

4.3
General planning considerations

Whilst there are a number of planning decisions which need to be taken before each lesson begins (see 4.4 below), there are some more general points which concern the overall approach to listening work and these have to be dealt with in advance.

4.3.1
A separate lesson, or part of a general lesson?

Is it your intention to have a separate listening lesson, where the main focus will be on listening practice? Or is listening to be integrated into one or more of the general language lessons? This may be something on which your school or department has a policy, but the answer must be taken into account when planning an overall schedule of listening work for a class.

There is growing support for the view that listening should play a central role in language teaching and that it should be integrated with other skills work. This does not mean, however, that you cannot plan parts of lessons, or even whole lessons, when the focus will be on listening. Indeed, it is often more practical to set aside a time for such work, perhaps so that it can be done in a quieter place, or at a quieter time, or when the students are less tired. And focussing on one skill does not mean, of course, that others must be rigorously excluded.

4.3.2
In the classroom, language lab or listening centre?

Again, practical considerations will often determine the location of the listening class, but you may sometimes be in a position to choose which of a variety of activities to do in the classroom and which in the language laboratory or listening centre.

In making the choice, bear in mind:

(a) that a teacher-spoken listening text is best done in a place where the students can see the teacher easily;
(b) that groupwork is often hard to arrange in a language laboratory;
(c) that, if students are to work alone, the language laboratory or the listening centre gives them privacy.

Consideration should also be given to whether the students will have control of their own playback systems, so that they can work at their own speed and go back over the listening text as often as they choose. And you will need to decide whether you intend all the students to work on the same text at the same time, or whether you can arrange for them to use different texts, depending perhaps on differing levels and interests.

Language laboratories which have supplies of tapes for listening are useful locations for individualised work, and even for some interactive work related to listening if they are spacious enough. Listening centres are even better in that they provide opportunities for students to use tapes as self-access study material, selecting topics that interest them at the level they can handle.

4.3.3 Equipment

Wherever the listening work is to be done, you will need to know what equipment is available to you, and to ensure that you can handle it efficiently.

Audio cassette recorders have greatly improved in quality in recent years, but you should not leave it to chance that a machine will be satisfactory at the time you decide to use it. Playing recordings on a poor quality machine, or on a machine which needs attention, leads to frustration for students and teachers alike. If a machine of adequate quality is not available, you would be best advised to do most of your listening work by using your own, or colleagues', 'live' voices.

During listening practice, one of the teacher's roles is to start and stop the recording, perhaps using the 'pause' button, to rewind the tape, etc. This role of 'technical operator' is an important one as the smoothness with which you use the equipment will significantly influence the atmosphere in which your students listen and how easy or difficult it will be for them to concentrate. You should never use equipment in a lesson until you are sure you can operate it efficiently and confidently.

4.3.4 Preparing recordings

If you intend to make recordings for class use, it is unlikely that there will be time and opportunity to plan and prepare even two or three recordings each week. Often, the enthusiasm and energy shown in the first three or four weeks of such a schedule tend to wane as the weeks go by, and either the quality deteriorates or the schedule breaks down. Quite remarkable tenacity is needed to keep to such a schedule when all the other lesson planning has to be done at the same time.

If you intend to record your own listening texts, to use, for example, alongside the established coursebook, then it is worth trying to organise and complete enough recordings for a number of weeks (perhaps a term/semester) in advance, as a major project. In this way, you will know that you have material which will be of an even quality to depend on.

4.3.5 The amount of time to be allocated to listening

Some schemes of work now require teachers to allot a certain percentage of the total lesson time to listening work. Some, however, do not. If you have no guidelines, you will have to decide for yourself what proportion of the week's total language-learning time should be devoted to listening work. This does not mean that listening will not be practised at other times, but it does mean making a commitment to concentrate on listening skills for a certain period each week. The time available, the location to be used, the level of the group, will all contribute to decisions about what listening work is possible and how you will be able to organise it.

4.3.6 The place of tests

Whether your students are expected to do examinations which include listening tests is a matter you cannot ignore in planning the listening work for a particular group. If an exam is looming, your students must be prepared for the kinds of tests which they will face, so their listening practice must include the types of exercise they will have to do. But this should not be to the exclusion of all other types, which contribute to the general development of listening skills and which therefore add to students' ability to do the exam successfully.

4.4
Before the lesson

There are a number of steps to take when planning the listening work for your class:

(a) *Choose the listening text* (see Chapter 10, 'Criteria for the selection of recorded material')

Even if you are using a prescribed set of listening materials, you may wish to take them out of sequence to match the topics/functions in the coursebook you are using.

(b) *Check that the activities are suitable* (see Chapters 5, 6 and 7 on pre-, while- and post-listening)

It is very important for the teacher to *listen to* the listening text, not just to read the transcript, to check both the text itself and whether the students will be able to do the activities. If you only look at the transcript, you may find when you get to the class that the recording is not clear at a particular point and your students cannot, therefore, do one of the tasks. This is particularly important if you are using a text with which you are not familiar and writing your own exercises. Recordings do not always give prominence to those parts of the discourse which you might expect to hear clearly from your reading of the transcript. Such things as speakers turning away from the microphone or noise in the background can cause unexpected problems.

(c) *Adjust the level of difficulty of the activities if you need to* (see Chapter 5, 'The pre-listening stage')

You may decide to do this by adding some answers on the handout the students are going to use. Or you can make a note for yourself of any extra pre-listening you feel you should introduce.

(d) *Consider whether the listening work you are planning will fill the time available*

If it is likely to be too little, plan what else you will do. This is especially important if you are going to work in the language laboratory, where some students will finish before others and will need further work to do.

If it turns out that you have too much work for the time available, what will you do about the rest? Set it for homework perhaps? Or abandon it? If you have to abandon some of the work, check whether the ground you planned to cover has been covered or whether you need to include some of it in a subsequent lesson.

(e) *Think about visual aids*

Are any essential or desirable? Some visual support is helpful for many students if only to remind them of ideas and language they may know but have temporarily forgotten.

(f) *Decide whether any special equipment will be needed*

Will the students need rulers, scissors, coloured pencils or anything else? If so, let them know in advance so that they can bring them along on the day they are needed.

(g) *Make up your mind what procedure you will adopt for the listening session*

– Will you use a recorded text or will you present the text yourself?
– Will you go through the whole thing without stopping? Will you want to use pauses? If so, it is useful to mark the transcript of the tape so that you will know where to stop the machine in class.
– How will you organise each stage? Will pre-listening work be done, for example, in pairs/groups or individually? (see Chapter 5)
– Will you replay the recording, or respeak the text, as often as your students ask you to? (see Chapter 6)
– Will you encourage the students to help each other at all stages or only, say, after the while-listening stage? (see Chapter 7)
– Will you want the students to write down any answers, or to make any notes?
– Will you do the corrections in class? (see Chapter 7)

(h) *If you are planning to present the listening text 'live', practise reading it aloud*

The quality of your presentation plays a large part in assisting and motivating the learners. Whilst it is a bad idea to rehearse to the point where your delivery becomes a wooden recitation, it is important to go through your text/notes to ensure that you can deliver it convincingly and reasonably naturally. You may also want to mark the places where you intend to pause or stop, or to annotate the text in other ways to assist you with your reading in class.

4.5
During the lesson

Most of the teacher's work associated with listening practice is done before the actual lesson. In class, the teacher must stand back and give the students time to think. Many teachers find this part of their role difficult and are inclined to proffer help too soon. The crucial thing is for the students to know that they can seek help from the teacher at any time and that the help will be given in a supportive manner, rather than as a correction.

You can create and maintain an encouraging class atmosphere by:

(a) *being available to give help whenever it is needed, but not inflicting help on those who do not need it. This may be at any stage during the lesson.*

(b) *encouraging the students to help each other, so that the emphasis is on the successful completion of the task(s) rather than on who got it 'right' or 'wrong'.*

(c) *not treating the activities as tests to be marked and scored.*

(d) *encouraging the students to alter their answers if they wish to, perhaps after listening for a second time.*

Some students, and even some teachers, have an aversion to 'messy' pages, particularly when using printed materials. You can suggest that your students write their answers in pencil, so that they can change them as often as they wish, or you can simply encourage them to cross out and replace answers if they want to.

(e) *encouraging students to jot down odd words, ideas and thoughts as they are doing their listening work.*

If the students own their own copies of the book, it is a good idea for them to jot things down on the pages to which they refer, as looking back and seeing their notes in context helps them to learn and remember new lexis and expressions.

(f) *suggesting that the students use dictionaries when it would prove helpful.*

Discussion of new lexis and the use of dictionaries can form a useful part of pre-listening work and teaches students how to find things out for themselves in the future when they will not have a teacher to depend on. However, it is important to limit this kind of work and to concentrate on those parts of the listening text which the students really have to understand in order to carry out the task(s). It should not turn into an explanation of every word in the text as this hinders, rather than assists, the development of the students' listening skills. On the other hand, there is no point in refusing to discuss the meaning of a word which a student has identified and asked about. In reality, no matter how well a teacher knows a group of students, and however thoroughly the lesson has been prepared, it often turns out that things which the teacher had identified as 'sticking points' cause less trouble than expected, whilst attention has to be given to things which the teacher thought would be no problem at all.

(g) *including lots of pair- and groupwork.*

The fact that every individual listens 'alone', and in a way which no other person can analyse, does not mean that listening tasks have to be done alone too. Indeed, discussion of different persons' perceptions of what was heard is a useful aid to improving listening skills. Checking and counter-checking of specific bits of a listening text gives a real reason for listening and encourages careful attention.

Where students have not formerly been successful, pair- and groupwork helps to remove some of the feelings of isolation and anxiety, and can make listening into a more pleasurable activity.

(h) *making listening work enjoyable.*

To listen attentively, students need to be at ease and calm and have a clearly defined purpose. It is very difficult to concentrate if one has no reason for listening (unless, of course, the content or the presentation is exceptionally interesting or exciting). This means that you should exploit every opportunity to give your students a sense of purpose, followed by a sense of achievement, in their listening work. And, having chosen suitable topics and planned activities, you should be ready to adjust your plans as you go through the lesson if you find that your students are not coping or are losing interest.

(i) *leaving out part of the work rather than rushing.*

There is a temptation, even for the most experienced teacher, to try to get something finished rather than give up part of the planned work (particularly if the group is in the language laboratory for its one scheduled hour of the week there). Even after a number of listening sessions with a particular group, it is difficult to judge how much you will do in one lesson. Generally speaking, it is better to omit something rather than to rush: because of the nature of listening, and the tendency for inexperienced listeners to panic, it is better to err on the side of giving too much time rather than speeding along.

(j) *giving immediate feedback.*

Students like to know how well they have performed the task and to discuss their efforts while the listening text is still fresh in their minds. Indeed, it is often useful to refer back to the passage and to replay parts of the recording (or respeak the text) to clarify points which emerge during feedback.

4.6 Conducting the lesson

Part of the teacher's role is to ensure that the lesson proceeds in an orderly and productive way so that the students feel secure and relaxed and unthreatened by the listening tasks. Following much the same sequence in each listening session helps students to know what is expected of them and thus reduces anxiety.

A good pattern for a listening session should include:

(a) the pre-listening stage, when the context of the listening text is established, the task(s) explained and assistance given/offered as necessary (see Chapter 5 for ideas);

(b) the while-listening stage, when the students listen to the passage (in some instances one section at a time) and attempt the while-listening activities (see Chapter 6 for ideas);

(c) a period when students discuss their responses, in pairs/groups, and help each other with the task;

(d) if necessary, a repeat listening, for students to continue/complete the activity or to check/clarify information they may have missed or think they may have got wrong;

(e) perhaps some further discussion between students, or some assistance from the teacher, leading if necessary to listening again to all or part(s) of the text;

(f) post-listening production of the 'acceptable' answers, either by the teacher or the class in general;

(g) consideration of the areas where students failed to understand or missed something and discussion of why this happened, playing through the text again, in whole or in part, if necessary;

(h) perhaps a post-listening extension activity (see Chapter 7 for ideas).

Conclusion

Teachers who make it clear that they believe in the value of listening work and who plan and conduct listening sessions in a purposeful way will find that their students grow in confidence and soon begin to experience the pleasure that listening successfully can bring.

Discussion

1 How do you 'rate' listening in the language curriculum? How do your colleagues feel about it?

2 Do you think your students would find it helpful if you explained to them, in their own language if necessary, something about how listening works? What would you want to tell them?

Exercises

1 Pay particular attention to what people are saying for a short time (about three minutes). As they speak, try to predict what is coming next and consciously consider how it is that you are able to make predictions (even if they are sometimes wrong). Could you heighten your students' awareness by asking them to do the same exercise?

2 Using 4.3 above as a checklist, go through the general planning considerations which apply in your teaching situation and decide whether there are any steps you need to take.

3 Go through the steps suggested in 4.4 above to plan just one listening session extra carefully. Having done this, consider whether there are any steps which you feel need attention in your future planning.

4 Compare the way you currently run listening sessions with the suggested sequence in 4.6. Is there anything in that section which you might incorporate into your approach?

PART 2

5

The pre-listening stage

There are very few occasions when people listen without having some idea of what they expect to hear. For example, when you go to the check-in desk at the airport, you have an idea of what the clerk will say. And when you meet an old friend, you probably know more or less what the opening words will be. But when students sit in a classroom and the teacher says 'Listen to this', and then switches on the cassette recorder or begins to read aloud, the students may have no idea what to expect. Even if the sounds and words they hear are not unfamiliar, they may still be unable to understand because they lack certain kinds of knowledge necessary for them to comprehend. Firstly, they may not know what the topic is or what the setting is or what the relationship between the speakers is. Secondly, even if the teacher has indicated what they are going to listen to – for example, two people talking about a particular topic – they may have insufficient grasp of the 'cultural framework' in which the speakers will speak and therefore will have no idea what is *meant*, even if they can understand (at least some of) the words.

It is unfair to plunge students straight into the listening text, even when testing rather than teaching listening comprehension, as this makes it extremely difficult for them to use the natural listening skills (which we all use in our native language) of matching what they hear with what they expect to hear and using their previous knowledge to make sense of it. So, before listening, students should be 'tuned in' so that they know what to expect, both in general and for particular tasks. This kind of preparatory work is generally described as 'pre-listening work' or just 'pre-listening'.

There will, of course, be odd occasions in real life on which listeners have little or no prior knowledge or expectation of what will be said and you can assist your students in coping with these situations too. However, it is helpful to focus at first on providing considerable pre-listening support so that the students can achieve a high level of success and thus become confident that they can listen effectively.

Pre-listening work can be done in a variety of ways and often occurs quite naturally when listening forms part of an integrated skills course. When planning lessons, time must be allocated for pre-listening activities and these activities should not be rushed.

5.2
Types of pre-listening activity

The words 'activity/activities' are used throughout this book to embrace the whole variety of things that might be done, in the classroom or outside it, in relation to listening texts. In the case of pre-listening activities, some of these are clearly preparation for listening (e.g. reading about a topic), while others might appear to be no more than the setting up of the while-listening activity. But it is important to note that in the very act of setting up the while-listening activity the students should be being helped to focus on what they are about to hear, and in this sense this is a pre-listening activity. Often, there is not a clear cut-off point between a pre-listening activity and the while-listening activity which follows it, so readers are urged to look upon the activities given as examples in this chapter as being closely linked with while-listening activities of the types described in the next chapter.

Pre-listening work can consist of a whole range of activities, including:

– the teacher giving background information;
– the students reading something relevant;
– the students looking at pictures;
– discussion of the topic/situation;
– a question and answer session;
– written exercises;
– following the instructions for the while-listening activity;
– consideration of how the while-listening activity will be done.

Each of these activities helps to focus the students' minds on the topic by narrowing down the things that the students expect to hear and activating relevant prior knowledge and already known language. For those without sufficient prior knowledge of the topic, such activities provide an opportunity to gain some (even if limited) knowledge which will help them to follow the listening text. In addition, it is likely that in this kind of pre-listening activity, students will actually use the words which they will shortly hear in the text. This 'bringing to the forefront' of known lexis and syntax will assist them when they come to match what they hear with their store of knowledge. And it is important to remember that pre-listening activities are needed just as much when the teacher is going to speak or read the listening text, although the nature and extent of the activities may be different in this case, and the distinction between pre- and while-listening work less clearly defined.

5.3
Authentic activities

It is often at the pre-listening stage that you can ensure that the listening activities, as well as the text itself, are made as realistic as possible. It is important not only for students to hear language which sounds natural, but also for them to have listening experiences which are as authentic as possible, i.e. to do the kinds of things which listeners do in real-life situations, and not merely do exercises on the language which is used.

It is impossible to provide truly authentic experiences for the students all the time. However, you can help to increase the sense of realism by providing information about when, where, by whom and to whom the words were spoken and by devising activities which might naturally emerge from those particular texts.

Many listening activities require the student to act as an eavesdropper, rather than as a participant in the interaction. This is a role which occurs less frequently in real life but is accepted as a teaching/learning strategy because it enables the student to practise listening to a wider range of language than might be experienced in face-to-face encounters in the classroom.

Whilst every attempt should be made to contextualise the texts presented to students and to give the listening work a degree of realism, it has to be accepted that this can often provide only an approximation of the situations which occur in real life. As Widdowson[1] says, 'The very fact that the foreign language makes its appearance in the contrived context of the classroom must inevitably undermine in some degree any authenticity it might naturally have. The pupils know perfectly well that they are being required to play a part in a kind of game. The crucial issue is whether the rules can be so devised that they will want to play, whether we can engage them in activities which are purposeful without being realistic so that they will willingly accept the artifice.'

5.4
The need for clear instructions

Making sure that the students know exactly what is required of them is an essential part of the pre-listening stage. All the students should understand what they have to do before you start to play, read or speak the listening text. Not knowing can cause students to 'switch off' and not attempt to do anything, and this in turn distracts those who are trying to perform the task.

When self-access materials are being used, the need for clear instructions is paramount as students who do not know precisely what to do may simply abandon the whole exercise.

Generally speaking, listening books produced for student use have clear, printed instructions. Even so, it is prudent to check that everyone has understood and is ready to begin, and to add any more instructions that may be required. You may decide, for example, to break an activity down into smaller steps and would then need to tell this to the class.

Students find it helpful if, when asked to identify a number of 'items' or to note a number of points from the listening text, they know in advance how many items or points they are expected to find. This bit of information seems to help them concentrate on the task and, afterwards, to give them a comforting sense of having achieved the objective, which in turn acts as a motivating force on future occasions.

Sometimes, students are asked to give answers to questions. You may need to specify whether very brief answers are satisfactory or whether more complete sentences are required. In general, for the purposes of listening skills development, it is better to accept the shortest possible answer: this shows whether or not the answer has been found and does not disadvantage the less able speaker or writer, who may have understood perfectly well but is not able to formulate a long answer.

Another important aspect of giving instructions is to ensure that, if a listening text is to be repeated a number of times, there is a clear and definite purpose for listening each time, and that all the purposes are not declared at the first run through. For example, before the first playing of a listening text, you might say 'We'll listen now and fill in the chart.' Then you might suggest that the students compare answers with a partner. Then you could replay the text, or maybe only part of it, after saying 'There seems to be some disagreement about . . . ., so let's listen again and check that part carefully. Change your answers if you want to.' Then you might have a brief discussion about what the answers are and what was actually said which gave the answers. This could be followed by a third playing, introduced by 'We all seem to have sorted it out now. Let's just run through again to check and change anything we still haven't got quite right.' The intention should be to help the students complete the various activities, to support them and encourage them, rather than to judge them and criticise them, as this will only reinforce any negative attitudes they may have towards listening work.

5.5 Teacher's books as a source of ideas

Although there is often little evidence of pre-listening work in published students' books, there are frequently suggestions in accompanying teacher's books. For this reason, it is advisable to check the teacher's book before embarking on preparations for a lesson, as you may well find that some, if not all, the work has been done for you by the author.

5.6 Factors which affect the choice of pre-listening activities

The choice of activities will depend on a number of factors, such as:

– the time available;
– the material available;
– the ability of the class;
– the interests of the class;
– the interests of the teacher;
– the place in which the work is being carried out;
– the nature and content of the listening text itself.

The last item on the list, 'the nature of the listening text itself', is very important when choosing activities. Some kinds of activity are simply not appropriate to some types of text and, in other instances, the text itself very naturally makes one type of activity especially appropriate.

Consider, for example, this situation:

You have selected a recorded listening text which consists of a two-minute conversation between a worried husband and wife. You have told your students that these parents have a twelve-year-old son, Peter, who has failed to come home from school. He is usually home around 4.30 pm. It is now 9 pm. Your class has had some experience of listening to dialogues, and you do not expect them to have major problems with individual words. Now you need to decide what you will do in the pre-listening stage of the lesson. A number of activities arise very naturally from this text. Here are some possibilities:

(a) The students, singly or in pairs or groups, could be asked to list some possible reasons for the non-appearance of Peter. To make it clear what you want them to do, you could ask for a number of possible answers to the question 'Why hasn't Peter come home?' or 'Why do you think Peter hasn't arrived home yet?' You will probably get answers like 'He's had an accident,' 'He's gone to his friend's house,' 'He's in hospital,' 'He's probably gone to the cinema.'

(b) The students, in pairs or groups, could be asked to discuss their views on whether a twelve-year-old should be out so late without his parents' permission. To start off the discussion, you might pose a question or two.

(c) The students could be asked to make a list of the possibilities now open to the parents. To get the activity started, you could ask 'What can the parents do?'/'What should the parents do now?' This time, you might expect answers like 'Go to the police,' 'Phone all his friends,' 'Wait at home,' 'Phone the school.'

(d) The students could be invited to speculate on what each of the parents is likely to say. You could help them to start thinking about this by asking 'How do you think the parents feel?' 'What do you think the mother is saying?' 'And the father?' The answers will probably generate some debate! Students might say 'She'll be worried,' 'The father will be blaming the mother (and vice versa),' 'She'll be saying "My poor boy! I should have gone to meet him,"' and so on.

Listening texts which naturally give rise to activities of this kind are particularly useful and are generally quite motivating for students.

5.7 Limiting pre-listening work

The level of difficulty of listening work can be adjusted by (a) the selection of less/more difficult texts or (b) the setting of less/more difficult tasks or (c) giving less/more support to the students.

By limiting the amount (and sometimes the type) of pre-listening activity, the task of listening can be made more difficult, and you may sometimes want to adjust the level of difficulty by varying the pre-listening work. However, this should not be done to the extent of making the listening unnatural by, for example, withholding information which would normally be known before listening.

It is possible, though often not very practicable, to vary the amount of pre-listening for different groups within a single class so that the more able are stretched while those who have difficulty can get support. One way to do this is to provide different handouts to different students, giving varied amounts of help. But this gives rise to two further difficulties: firstly, the students who need most support in listening may be slower at assimilating printed material too, and so the more able students have to wait or be found some other occupation; and secondly, unless your class consists of students who are sufficiently adult to appreciate that they need more help (because they are new to the class, for example), treating some students differently from others has to be handled with great care.

5.8 Ideas for pre-listening activities

This section offers a selection of ideas for pre-listening work, with examples taken from various published sources. The examples come from materials designed for a range of levels, but the basic idea of each activity can be adapted for use with other texts at other levels.

The one activity which teachers are urged *not* to use is going through the tapescript bit by bit explaining the 'difficult' words to the students.

5.8.1
Looking at
pictures before
listening

This activity can be used when students are not able to read English, but does not, of course, have to be limited to that situation.

Students are asked to look at a picture (or pictures). You may want to assist by checking that the students can name the items which will feature in the listening text. This can be done by question and answer or by general or group discussion. Giving long lists of unknown words and long explanations should be avoided as this does not help the students to listen naturally.

Pre-listening 'looking and talking about' is an effective way of reminding students of lexis which may have been forgotten (or perhaps never really known) and of focussing attention on the topic to be listened to.

In the following example, discussion in pairs gives the students a chance to hear and use some of the language they will meet in the dialogues they subsequently hear.

EXAMPLE

2

Work

1 People at work

Task 1

Look at these photographs of people at work. What do you think they are saying? Discuss your answers in pairs.

From Rob Nolasco *Listening* (Elementary), page 8. Oxford University Press 1987

5.8.2
Looking at a list of
items/thoughts/etc
before listening

This type of activity is particularly helpful for practising newly learned
vocabulary with early learners. The list should not consist merely of words
which may prove difficult, but should have some purpose of its own in the
total listening activity. It could, for example, be a list on which certain
items/ideas will be ticked/circled/underlined at the while-listening stage. It
should be an integral part of the listening activity as far as the students are
concerned but can be exploited as pre-listening material by the teacher.

Looking before listening removes the stress of suddenly hearing
something forgotten or half forgotten and thus being distracted from the next
part of the listening text. Presenting the list in the order in which the
words/phrases/statements occur in the text makes while-listening exercises
easier. If the students are getting too casual, or simply finding the task too
easy, the level of difficulty can be increased by putting the list in random
order. Another variant, which provides useful practice for students whose
alphabet differs from the English alphabet, is to put the items on the list in
alphabetical order.

A checking exercise is made more difficult for the listener if the list
contains some 'distractors', i.e. words or phrases which are not referred to at
all in the listening text, or are not needed to produce answers. Many
examinations make extensive use of distractors, even to the extent of
including words and phrases which are very similar indeed in sound to the
'correct' answers so that the examinee is severely tested. In time, students
who wish to take exams will need to get used to this. But in order not to
discourage the students, they should be used sparingly until most of them are
reasonably confident listeners.

This example is taken from a 'revision' unit and presents the students
with language they have already learned. A quick pre-listening look at the list
will probably refresh their memories and make them ready to listen.

EXAMPLE

🔲 Listen

Listen to Jenny and Mickey talking about jobs
in the house. Look at the list below and tick the
jobs which they do.

take the rubbish out	tidy her/his room
go shopping	wash up
make the beds	lay the table
take the dog for a walk	do some cooking

TRANSCRIPT

INTERVIEWER: Tell me, Jenny, do you ever help your mother at home?
JENNY: Yes, I do quite a lot really.
INTERVIEWER: What sort of things do you do?
JENNY: Well, I do the washing up and make the beds and things like that.
INTERVIEWER: Washing up, make the beds?
JENNY: Yeah, and whatever . . .
INTERVIEWER: Every day?
JENNY: Well, not every day. Usually it's done but whenever it's sort of . . . not done. I just do it.
INTERVIEWER: What about laying the table?
JENNY: Um, well, I usually do that as Mum's dishing up the dinner.

INTERVIEWER: And do you have a pet?
JENNY: Yes, I have a dog.
INTERVIEWER: So how much do you exercise it? Do you have to take the dog for walks and things like that?
JENNY: Yeah, I usually take her for a long walk on Sunday.
INTERVIEWER: You don't take her every day for a walk?
JENNY: No, 'cos it gets dark before five.
INTERVIEWER: So it's really just once a week.
JENNY: Yes . . . proper walk.
INTERVIEWER: Mickey. Tell me. Do you ever help your mother in the house? (ctd)

From Brian Abbs and Ingrid Freebairn *Discoveries* Student's Book 1, page 80; transcript from Teacher's Book, pages 121–122. Longman 1986

5.8.3
Making lists of possibilities/ideas/ suggestions/etc

When a listening text contains lists, even short lists, of possibilities/ideas/suggestions or whatever, it is often a good idea to use list-*making* as the pre-listening activity and then the students can use their own lists as the basis for a while-listening activity. The great advantage of students making lists for themselves is that their lists can only contain words and expressions which they know, or which they learn by asking for help as they make their lists. Any checking-type activity carried out while listening can then be limited to matching with known language. This increases the likelihood of the students succeeding with the task and is therefore motivating, particularly for less able students.

Pre-listening list-making is a good pair or group activity and can be done in a relaxed way because there are no right answers for what should be on the lists. It is best, certainly at the beginning of a course when students are not used to this kind of work, to use list-making for subjects about which most people are likely to have plenty of ideas, e.g. 'items you'd like to own', 'things children are afraid of', 'people you'd like to meet', 'favourite things to eat'.

5.8.4
Reading a text before listening

Frequently, students can be asked to read a text before listening and then to check certain facts while listening. This type of activity is popular with students who feel more secure when they have a printed text in front of them.

To be ready to check when they hear the listening text, students need to read quite carefully. Concentration on the written text brings the language which is likely to be heard to mind. Unfortunately, reading in advance in this way may leave those who have learned their English mainly from the printed word still in difficulty when they are listening, as they may be unable to connect the sounds which they hear with the words which they have seen printed on the page. If this is the case, you can assist by contriving, during the pre-listening stage, to speak some of the words which are printed and which you know will occur in the listening text.

In this example, students are asked to fill the gaps in the text as they read it through at the pre-listening stage and then to check their answers as they listen to the recorded version.

EXAMPLE

Unit 24

Describing things

A Medium-sized, not small

The language of descriptions; listening and speaking practice; pronunciation.

1 Some people were asked to describe the butterflies from memory. Here are some of the things they said about one of the butterflies. Can you complete the sentences with words from the box? (There are too many words.) When you have finished, listen to the recording and check your answers. Which butterfly were the people describing?

'.............-sized, brown ...., black markings with a bright red –'

'Well, er ...., er brown, some white, on the wing-tips I think, and, er, yes, medium-............, not small, not ....-large like a peacock, er, can't remember anything ....'

'I don't think I could .... anything to that. No, that's .... what I'd say, that it was red and white, sort of ....-red, with two white eyes in the larger wings.'

'I think it has a sort of pattern of ...., doesn't it, of some sort, in the sort of – at the top of its wing.'

'There's a red – black and red .... going along the top and there's a .... of white blobs somewhere.'

'The actual bulk of it was brownish, with red on the .... of the wings, the fore-wings. I think there was eyes on the lower wings, in the ...., and there's white as well.'

about	add	background	centre	couple
dots	else	extra	medium	orangey
outside	red	sized	stripe	

2 Close your book and describe one of the other butterflies from memory.

Peacock

Red Admiral

Small Tortoiseshell

From Michael Swan and Catherine Walter *The Cambridge English Course* Student's Book 3, page 98. Cambridge University Press 1987

5.8.5
Reading through
questions (to be
answered while
listening)

Many listening activities require students to answer questions based on information they hear. It is very helpful indeed for the students to see the questions before they begin listening to the text. Not only do they then know what they have to seek from the text, but they also benefit from the reading itself, as explained in 5.8.4. above. In addition, the type of question asked gives an indication of the kind of thing that is likely to be heard. The students' task is made more difficult if the list of questions is jumbled, as their expectations of the order of presentation will not be met.

In this particular example, the questions follow the order in which the answers will be found in the listening text. They are also evenly spread, so that students need to listen carefully throughout.

EXAMPLE

2. Telephone call – a rush job

a) You will hear a telephone call received by Midland International Transport, a firm of hauliers based in Coventry. Read the following questions through before you listen, and then answer them after hearing the conversation to be sure that you have understood all the details.

   i) Which company does the caller, Mr. Daniels, represent?
   ii) Why does Mr. Daniels' firm require a rush job?
   iii) Why does his firm require delivery by a specific day?
   iv) What factors does Mr. Samson think will increase the cost of the delivery?
   v) Why does Mr. Daniels say that he will contact the French supplier?

TRANSCRIPT

SAMSON: Good morning, Midland International.

DANIELS: Morning. Is that Mr. Samson?

SAMSON: Speaking.

DANIELS: It's Tom Daniels here, from Coventry Engineering.

SAMSON: Good morning, Mr. Daniels, what can we do for you?

DANIELS: It's a rush job, I'm afraid. We need some machine parts from France. Our supplier in Paris let us down at the last minute.

SAMSON: I see. When would you need them by?

DANIELS: This Saturday. We need to fit the parts on the machine this Saturday so that we can get on with production from Monday. Do you think you can do it?

SAMSON: Well, let's see . . . Today's Thursday . . . I could send a driver off tonight . . . It can be done. But we'd have to send an empty lorry over there as we are rather short of time. Couldn't you have someone in France put the parts on a ferry so that we could collect them at the dock?

DANIELS: No, we've had enough trouble already. We'd rather know exactly where the parts are. We can't afford another mistake. Now, can you do it?

SAMSON: Well, I suppose so, but I can't give you a definite idea of the price at the moment. We'd probably need to send a thirty-five foot trailer, both ways perhaps, on the most expensive ferry crossing. It'll be above our usual rates . . .

DANIELS: We'll talk about the cost afterwards. The main thing is to get those machine parts here by Saturday, or the cost in lost time will be much higher. I can imagine what our Production Manager would say. Now, I'll get on to the suppliers to make sure the parts are ready for despatch and they've got their documents organised, and then I'll give you a ring back to tell you where to find their depot and give you the other details you need. . . .

From M Poté, D Wright, A Esnol, G Lees, R Soulieux *A Case for Business English* Student's Book, page 24; transcript from Teacher's Book, pages 18–19. Pergamon 1985

**5.8.6
Labelling a picture**

This is another activity which can be used to revise already known language. It is suitable for pairwork and can generate a lot of discussion.

The pre-listening part consists of endeavouring to label a picture or diagram. Even if the students are able to complete all the labels before they hear the listening text, it is still a good activity as they can listen and check whether they were right and get the feeling of satisfaction which comes from immediate feedback.

If you feel that there are some words needed for the labelling which are really too difficult for your class, you can fill them in before the lesson, as it is unsatisfactory to finish a labelling exercise with some parts of the picture/diagram unlabelled.

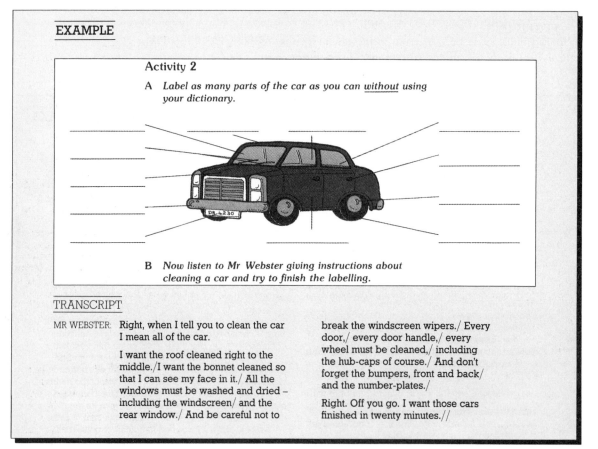

EXAMPLE

Activity 2

A *Label as many parts of the car as you can without using your dictionary.*

B *Now listen to Mr Webster giving instructions about cleaning a car and try to finish the labelling.*

TRANSCRIPT

MR WEBSTER: Right, when I tell you to clean the car I mean all of the car.

I want the roof cleaned right to the middle./ I want the bonnet cleaned so that I can see my face in it./ All the windows must be washed and dried – including the windscreen/ and the rear window./ And be careful not to break the windscreen wipers./ Every door,/ every door handle,/ every wheel must be cleaned,/ including the hub-caps of course./ And don't forget the bumpers, front and back/ and the number-plates./

Right. Off you go. I want those cars finished in twenty minutes.//

From Mary Underwood *Better Listening 2*, page 32; transcript from Teacher's Book, pages 41–42. Oxford University Press, Hong Kong, 1985

**5.8.7
Completing part of
a chart**

This activity can get the students involved in a personal way if they are invited to fill in their own views, judgements or preferences. It is a popular type of activity, perhaps because it is a challenge and an opportunity for students to compare their views and judgements with other people's. How far it assists students in matching the printed word with the heard word depends on the quantity and relevance of the writing used in the chart.

In this example, the information is presented in jumbled order, and so students need to move up and down the printed list quite rapidly. A shorter list would be needed for lower level students.

EXAMPLE

Exercise 16 Do you know when these things were invented or discovered? Write your answers in Column A – then listen to the tape, and write the correct answer in Column B. It's not easy!

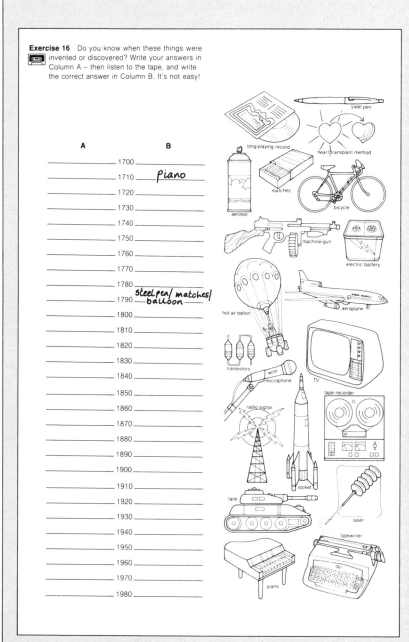

	A	B
1700		
1710		*Piano*
1720		
1730		
1740		
1750		
1760		
1770		
1780		
1790		*steel pen / matches / balloon*
1800		
1810		
1820		
1830		
1840		
1850		
1860		
1870		
1880		
1890		
1900		
1910		
1920		
1930		
1940		
1950		
1960		
1970		
1980		

TRANSCRIPT

. . . an Italian, Bartolomeo Christofori, invented the piano in 1709, and seventy years later, in 1780, the steel pen replaced the traditional quill pen. The 1780s saw the introduction of matches into Britain; these were well known in China, but this was the first time they had been seen in the West.

The Montgolfier brothers flew the first air balloon in 1783, and the early 1800s saw the invention of the electric battery. A form of machine-gun was invented in the early 1860s, and the first *efficient* typewriter was produced in the late sixties. An important invention, the microphone, appeared in 1877. This was to have a great effect on modern communications, as was Sturley's safety bicycle, built in the early 1880s. Marconi sent the first radio signal in 1897 and the tape recorder, which wasn't really a *tape* recorder, because it used *wire*, not *tape*, appeared two years later in 1899.

The Wright brothers became famous with their newly-developed aeroplane, which first flew in 1903, and during the First World War, the tank was produced in 1914. Television made its appearance in 1926, although the technology used in television had been known for the previous forty years. The rocket appeared six years later, in 1932. The aerosol was invented in 1941, and the transistor in the mid-forties, just before the first long-playing record, which appeared in 1948. Scharlow and Townes produced the first laser in 1950, and in 1967 Dr Christian Barnard made medical history by transplanting the first human heart.

From Steve Elsworth *Count Me In*, page 21; transcript from page 38. Longman 1982

5.8.8
Predicting/
speculating

Predicting precisely what the speaker will say next is a while-listening activity, but predicting/speculating in a more general way can be a pre-listening activity. Students can be told something about the speaker(s) and the topic and then asked to suggest what they are likely to hear in the listening text. This is a useful activity with advanced students and adult students who are perhaps more interested in speculating on the likely behaviour of individuals in particular situations.

This example invites students to speculate on what will be said, and thus provides them with the opportunity to call to mind and perhaps make some of the possible utterances themselves.

EXAMPLE

2. **Mary and Mr. Pearson**
Background information: Mary has worked for the sales department of a furniture company for over ten years. Recently she applied for the position of head of the sales department at the company.
Mr. Pearson, the head of the company, chose a person named Jack Bridgeman for the job instead of Mary. Mary thinks she should get the promotion instead. She goes to talk to Mr. Pearson. She wants Mr. Pearson to change his decision.

What do you think Mr. Pearson will say?

a. If you think you can handle the job, I'll change my decision and give the job to you.

b. We think we made the best decision. We're not going to change it.

c. Please talk to Jack and decide together who should get the new job.

From Michael Rost *Strategies in Listening*, page 69. Lateral Communications, San Francisco, 1986

5.8.9
Previewing the
language which
will be heard in
the listening text

There are sometimes occasions when you have a listening text which provides a good example of the use of particular language forms in an 'authentic' situation and which you want to use because your class has recently studied these forms. Although you will not wish to neglect the content, nor to use an uninteresting topic, you may want to focus on the language itself. In this case, a preview of the language might be the most appropriate form of pre-listening activity. This can be done either through discussion initiated by the teacher or by using prompts in the form of a written text.

In this example, students are presented with printed lists of expressions and the functional language which they will hear.

EXAMPLE

 INSTRUCTIONS

PREVIEW

Do you know these expressions?

APPLICATION FORM ITEMS

intended date of arrival	monthly/yearly salary
means of travel	deductions/taxes
port of arrival	current debts
purpose of visit	
	bill to someone
occupation	book catalogue
working hours	

FUNCTIONAL LANGUAGE

Could you help me . . .	How do I fill this in?
I don't understand how to . .	I don't understand this item . . .
What does . . . mean?	Is that all?
I'm having trouble . . .	How do I find that out?

From Michael Rost *Strategies in Listening*, page 31. Lateral Communications, San Francisco, 1986

5.8.10
Informal teacher talk and class discussion

This is a very common form of pre-listening activity, particularly when students are about to hear a recorded text. Teachers generally give their students some background information, begin to talk about the topic and indicate what the students should expect to hear. It does, however, require preparation as you need to know in advance what must be included in this talk, otherwise it is easy to go off at a tangent and fail to clarify or establish significant points. There is also a temptation to over-assist and to give too much away, so that by the time the actual listening text is played the students are bored and no longer want to listen. On the other hand, you can use this time to motivate the students by making them feel that the actual listening text is really interesting/exciting/amazing. Some teacher's books provide suggestions for this type of introduction to a listening text, but the best ideas often come from the teacher, who, in any case, is able to adjust the nature and level of the talk/discussion to suit the students.

5.9
Pre-listening as an integral part of listening work

The pre-listening activities described in 5.8 above should not be seen as isolated activities. Many pre-listening activities, as is apparent from the examples, are part of a continuum of activity which flows naturally into the while-listening stage. It is much better, therefore, if the pre-listening work is done immediately prior to the listening and *not* completed in a previous lesson, when many of the benefits described in 5.8 would be lost. Pre-listening work is the 'build-up' to the actual listening and serves not only to assist with comprehension but also to motivate students to *want* to listen. Separating the two activities is like somebody warming up for a race and then running the race itself some days later!

5.10
How pre-listening features in integrated skills work

Pre-listening can consist of reading, writing, speaking or all three. It provides opportunities for listening to be integrated with the other parts of the students' work. You could, for example, ask your students to read a short extract from a newspaper giving details of, say, a recent fire in the neighbourhood, and then ask them to listen to the same bit of news as it is reported on radio. Pre-listening and while-listening exercises could be carried out, and then the students could be asked to write a description of another fire (real or imagined) as homework. Alternatively, for a lower level class, you could ask the students, in pairs, to write down at least six words they might expect to hear when somebody talks about a fire at a house. This activity, of course, also provides an opportunity for students to practise speaking. Then they could hear the news item and after that see the text.

This kind of integrated skills approach provides opportunities for the students to use language in the way in which it is used in real life, and enables them to associate written and spoken language with language read and heard.

Discussion

1 If you were studying a foreign language, what would be the two or three main things you would want to know before beginning to listen to a text in that language?
2 Do you think that one or two of the types of pre-listening activity described in this chapter are more suitable for your students than the other types? If so, which ones are they? And why are they more suitable?

Exercises

1 Look at four or five listening exercises in some published material and decide whether you find the pre-listening work appropriate for one of your groups of students.
2 Take two or three examples of published listening exercises and produce what you believe would be better pre-listening activities for your students than the ones suggested in the books.
3 Examine the instructions given for these same exercises and consider whether you would wish to amend them in any way. If so, produce your amendments.

References

1 Professor H Widdowson, in an address to the Joint Council of Languages Association Conference in 1984 entitled 'Authentic versus Purposeful Activities'

6

The while-listening stage

6.1
**The purpose of
while-listening
activities**

While-listening activities are what students are asked to do during the time
that they are listening to the text. As far as listening comprehension (i.e.
listening for meaning) is concerned, the purpose of while-listening activities is
to help learners develop the skill of eliciting messages from spoken language.

There are, of course, other reasons why students need to listen to the
language they are studying, the main one being to learn to recognise how it
sounds (the pronunciation of words, the stress, the rhythm, the intonation) so
that they can use what they hear as a model for their own speech. This facet
of listening is not within the scope of this book, but is dealt with in detail in
Teaching English Pronunciation, by Joanne Kenworthy (Longman 1987).

Because it is important for students to know how the language sounds in
order to develop their listening comprehension skills, some early listening
work which focusses on this aspect is essential. It enables students to begin to
appreciate such things as the differences which exist between the
pronunciation of words when spoken within utterances and when spoken in
isolation (e.g. the use of weak syllables in continuous speech), and the stress
and rhythm of the language. In cases where students have already learned
some English but have had very limited exposure to the *spoken* language, it is
also important to make them aware of the relationship (or lack of any
apparent relationship!) between the written word and its spoken form.

When developing the skills of listening for comprehension is the aim,
while-listening activities must be chosen carefully. Activities which do no
more than test whether or not the listener has understood and which simply
produce 'right/wrong' answers will soon discourage all but the most
enthusiastic learner. There is a place for the testing of listening
comprehension, but this should not be the purpose of every listening practice
session.

People listening in their own language engage (though not usually
consciously) in prediction, at both macro and micro levels, matching what is

actually said with what they expect to hear, and interpreting the overall meaning of each utterance, which may not always be the same as the superficial meaning of the words. To help non-native listeners learn to apply these skills, which they have and use when listening in their own languages, we must have listening activities which give practice in prediction, matching and interpretation.

The 'macro' level of prediction (i.e. deciding what, in general, is likely to be said) is one of the purposes of pre-listening activities (see Chapter 5, section 5.8.8), but at the 'micro' level (i.e. deciding what words or ideas will follow immediately) prediction occurs at the while-listening stage. Matching is related to prediction in that the listener makes a series of predictions (generally without being conscious of doing so) and then matches them against what is actually said. The two activities seem to go on concurrently as one part is being matched while other micro predictions are being made. At the same time, interpretation has to be carried out, as the interpretation of one part of a message can affect the listener's prediction of what the next part will be. Sometimes, a listener fails to interpret something that is said and later remarks, 'I didn't realise what he meant at the time,' indicating that he/she has sorted out the message at some later stage. Sometimes, interpretation at the macro level is a post-listening activity when the overall meaning or interpretation of a message can be thought about at leisure.

Good while-listening activities help learners find their way through the listening text and build upon the expectations raised by pre-listening activities.

6.2
The nature of while-listening activities

6.2.1
Interest

While-listening activities should be interesting, so that students feel they want to listen and carry out the activities. Part of the interest can stem from the topic and the content of what is said, and the listening text should be chosen with the interests of the students in mind (see Chapter 10, 'Criteria for the selection of recorded material').

Many learners enjoy material with a 'local' flavour rather more than texts set in some remote (and unimaginable) context. For this reason, even quite mundane topics should be given some local relevance when possible in order to make them more familiar and motivating.

Another kind of interest is generated by activities which are in themselves interesting and satisfying to do. Most people enjoy trying to complete puzzles or solve problems and this fact can be exploited in the design of the activities. It is important, however, that this kind of activity is not too long and laborious and does not involve doing the same kind of thing over and over again. For example, for most people, three small crossword puzzles on different occasions are far more satisfying to do than one very large one which occupies a lot of time on just one occasion.

6.2.2
Levels of difficulty

While-listening activities should be things which most people *can* do. Failure here very rapidly leads to demotivation, and activities with potential 'sticking points', where students are likely to get into difficulties, should be used very sparingly in the early stages. In time, of course, it will be necessary to include activities which present potential 'sticking points', so that students learn not to be put off and to persevere in spite of the problems.

Activities which depend mainly on previously held knowledge are often not suitable for classroom while-listening work, as the level of knowledge may vary considerably within the group and those with more knowledge will succeed while those with less knowledge, but perhaps with greater listening skills, will not. Another problem with knowledge-based activities is that a great deal of time may be used in filling gaps in people's knowledge, and this can mean that (a) less time is spent on the actual listening work, and (b) students who already 'know' may lose interest. For these reasons, it is better to use activities where the solutions lie within the listening text and result from successful listening.

The level of difficulty of a while-listening activity can be adjusted by giving or withholding support. This can be done at the pre-listening stage (see Chapter 5, section 5.7), or at the while-listening stage.

Consider this situation in a classroom:

(a) The teacher says to the class 'I'm going to play you an incomplete sentence and I want you to try to complete it. Are you ready? Listen.'

(b) The teacher then presses the 'start' button on the cassette recorder and the students hear: 'Her children are now about six and four, and she has gone back. . .'.

(c) No student is able to complete the sentence. Why not? They say they didn't hear it clearly, or that they failed to grasp what the speaker was saying, or that they are 'lost' because they are not sure what is happening.

(d) The teacher then provides some background information and a context for the utterance. 'Actually, this woman is talking about whether women with children should go out to work or whether they should stay at home and look after their children. She is explaining what has happened in the case of a particular friend of hers.'

(e) The students are then given a second chance to try to complete the sentence. This time they are ready for what they are about to hear.

(f) The teacher replays the incomplete sentence: 'Her children are now about six and four, and she has gone back. . .'.

(g) The students now know what to expect (and in this particular example are actually hearing the incomplete utterance for the second time), and so many are able to make a reasonable guess at how the sentence will end.

(h) At this stage, the teacher might decide to offer more help, so that any students still having difficulty will have an even greater chance of succeeding (and incidentally those who think they have now got the answer will have a chance to check it). The teacher displays (on the blackboard or overhead projector):

    A to work
    B to her mother
    C to reading a lot

and says 'I'll play it again, and you choose which one it is – A, B or C.'

(i) The teacher plays the tape a third time and, in all probability, the majority of the class will have found the answer.

This sequence illustrates one way in which you can withhold or offer support. It is almost always necessary to give some indication of context if the students are to be kept interested in listening, but the amount of information given can be varied and the amount and type of help with the activities themselves can also be varied depending on the needs of the group being taught.

Some while-listening activities are successful with groups of varying levels of ability and provide a challenge for the more advanced students whilst not discouraging those who only achieve limited success.

In the ideas for while-listening activities in 6.4, attention is drawn to a number of ways in which support can be given by the careful choice of the type of activity.

6.2.3
Lack of complications

There are a number of things which can make while-listening work frustrating and demotivating and these should certainly be avoided. The most basic one is that it is extremely difficult to listen and write at the same time, particularly in a foreign language and when what is to be written is not exactly the words being spoken. It is unreasonable to expect students with limited listening experience or knowledge of English to write anything more than a two or three word response during a while-listening activity. Indeed, even this can be too much if the students have difficulty with writing, spelling or understanding what they hear or what they are supposed to be doing.

For this reason, while-listening work should be 'simple' – in the sense that it should be easy to handle. It should provide opportunities for students who listen well, but who may be less strong in other skills, to succeed. Exercises which require students to check/tick, draw, circle, etc make good while-listening activities and should not be rejected because of their simple structure. It is important to remember that the purpose is to assist concentration and to guide the listener through the text, not to test the ability to make correct sentences based on the content of the listening text.

Another type of activity which can be frustrating is the one which requires the listener to put a large number of sentences in the correct order according to what is heard. The difficulty is that it is often not until the end that the listener can be sure of having sorted everything out. This does not mean that 'sorting' exercises should not be done, but it does mean that they should contain a limited number of items, that 'trick' items which create potential confusion should not be included, and that the listeners should be allowed (even encouraged) to make their first attempts while- and post-listening, and then listen to the whole thing again to confirm or alter the order chosen.

The same kind of frustration sometimes occurs with true/false questions or multiple-choice questions. They must be designed in such a way that they can be completed at specific points while listening, and should not depend on the listener, who has lots more true/false or multiple-choice questions to tackle, having to retain information over long stretches of listening time in order to establish the answer. Again, some true/false and multiple-choice questions are more suitable as post-listening work when the listener has time to reflect (but see Chapter 7, section 7.1 on the disadvantages of this kind of post-listening activity).

6.3
Factors which affect the choice of while-listening activities

In addition to the factors listed in Chapter 5, section 5.6, which apply equally to while-listening activities, other points need to be considered when selecting while-listening activities. They include:

(a) the possibilities for varying the level of difficulty if required (see 6.2.2 above);

(b) the inconvenience of carrying out activities which require individuals to give their responses orally in the classroom. This kind of work is best done in a language laboratory. Classroom while-listening activities generally have to be limited to those which can be done without the need for each student to respond by speaking, although of course a great deal of listening occurs when a teacher speaks to a class or an individual, and then some kind of spoken response is made by the students without causing disturbance and preventing others from listening;

(c) whether the work is to be done by the students with the teacher present or whether it is to be done as private study, either in a listening centre or at home. This will influence the teacher's choice of activity as he/she may want

– to give different students different work according to their levels of ability;
– to provide additional instructions/clarification for work to be done away from the classroom; or
– to select activities which generate little or no marking;

(d) whether or not the while-listening activities generate material or ideas which might be used for other, post-listening work, and if so, whether the teacher wishes to make use of these.

6.4
Ideas for while-listening activities

This section offers a selection of ideas for while-listening work, with examples taken from various published sources. As in the case of the pre-listening selection in Chapter 5, the examples come from materials designed for a range of levels, but the basic idea of each activity can be adapted for use with other texts at other levels.

6.4.1
Marking/checking items in pictures.

Having carried out some pre-listening work using a picture, students are then asked to respond to various stimuli (questions/statements) by marking things on the picture.

The teacher who has checked through the actual listening text in advance (preferably by listening to it, not just by reading through the transcript) will have used the pre-listening stage to introduce any lexis or expressions which the students are not familiar with or need reminding about, so that the chances of everyone succeeding with the task will be enhanced (see Chapter

5, section 8.1). There are many activities which fall into this category: identifying people and things, marking items mentioned by the speaker, marking errors, checking details, marking choices, etc.

    This type of while-listening activity is good for helping students to focus on the listening itself, because they are not distracted by the need to try to write down words.

EXAMPLE

5 Finding out the house rules

Listening

Put a cross on the picture where the rule is being broken. Make brief notes of each rule.

TRANSCRIPT

JUDY: Well it's a lovely room. It's quite a nice size.
LANDLADY: Oh yes. It's a good-sized room and it's well-furnished.
JUDY: Yes. Yes I can see that. Erm . . . is there anything that I should know?
LANDLADY: Well, I don't allow the cat to go upstairs at all.
JUDY: Oh? Not at all.
LANDLADY: No, absolutely not. I don't like cats upstairs [Oh right.] And I don't allow people to smoke in bedrooms.
JUDY: Oh no, no I agree with that. I don't smoke anyway.
LANDLADY: And . . . erm . . . I don't allow people to stick pictures up on the walls with sellotape. [Oh?] Well you see, when you take the picture down the sellotape leaves . . . erm . . . a mark on the paper.

JUDY: Oh I see. Can I use blu-tack or something?
LANDLADY: Oh yes. Something like that [Oh right] is quite acceptable. [Lovely] And there are just two more things [Oh] if you don't mind. [Yes.] If you do go out, would you please remember to close the window.
JUDY: Right. I'll do that.
LANDLADY: And there's the kettle here, as you can see [Yes] but when you boil the kettle could you please put it on the floor and not on the chest of drawers?
JUDY: Oh I see. Does it make a mark or something?
LANDLADY: Yes it would probably leave a mark.
JUDY: Oh right. I'll do that then.
LANDLADY: Is . . . is that all right?
JUDY: Well it sounds very fair. Thank you very much.
LANDLADY: Yes all right. [OK] Good.

From Lesley Blundell and Jackie Stokes *Task Listening*, page 10. Cambridge University Press 1981

6.4.2
Which picture?

Students hear a description or a conversation and have to decide, from the selection offered, which picture is the 'right' one. The most common pictures used are drawings/photos of people or scenes, indoors or out of doors. This is an activity where the level of difficulty can be changed both by the degree of similarity or contrast between the pictures and by the level of sophistication of the description/conversation.

There are many examples of straightforward identification activities, but this one is more demanding and depends on the students interpreting what they hear and matching it with the pictures.

<u>EXAMPLE</u>

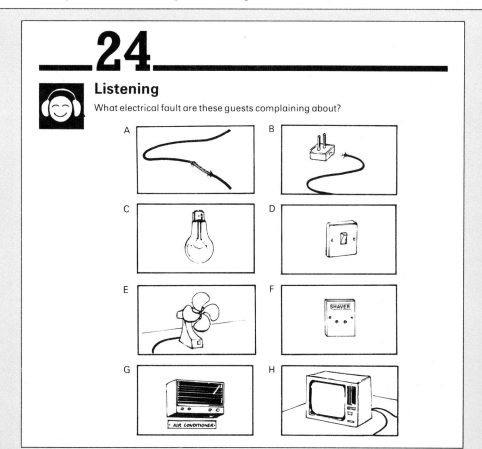

_24_

Listening

What electrical fault are these guests complaining about?

A   B   C   D   E   F   G   H

TRANSCRIPT

1. I can't get my shaver to work. I think it's the socket.
2. Could you have someone replace the light bulb in my room?
3. The plug's come off the bedside lamp. Could you get someone to fix it?
4. Look I'm absolutely sweltering in that room. When are you going to do something about the A.C?
5. I'd love to look at the telly, but I'm not getting any picture.
6. I can't turn the light off. The switch is faulty.
7. That fan is supposed to rotate, isn't it? Well, it won't.
8. The lamp flex is worn and you can see the bare wires. That's very dangerous.

From Shiona Harkness and Michael Wherly *You're Welcome!* Unit 24; transcript from Teacher's Book, page 23. Edward Arnold 1984

6.4.3
Storyline picture
sets

Two or three sets of, usually, three or four pictures are presented to the students who then listen to a story, either read by the teacher or on tape, and try to decide which set of pictures represents the story.

    This activity generally depends on each student having the sets of pictures in a book or on a work-sheet as it can be difficult to display the pictures in a satisfactory way for all to see.

    It is important that the differences between the picture sets occur near the end of the sequence, as the students may well stop listening as soon as they have made up their minds about which is the correct set.

EXAMPLE

A Listen to the story. Then choose "a" or "b" as the correct drawing for the story. Circle "a" or "b".

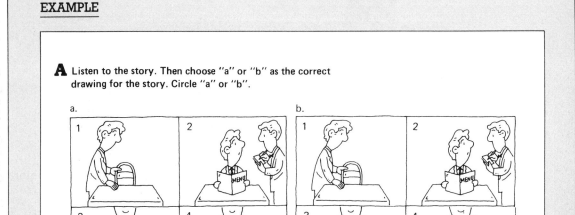

TRANSCRIPT

Last night I went into a restaurant. It was an Italian restaurant. I sat down. The waiter came to me and gave me a menu. I looked at the menu, then I ordered spaghetti and a salad. The waiter didn't say anything. I waited for about 15 minutes, then the waiter brought me a hamburger. He put the hamburger in front of me, and I said 'No, this isn't what I ordered.' So he took the hamburger away and I waited for 15 more minutes and then he brought me the spaghetti.

From Hiroshi Asano, Munetsugu Uruno and Michael Rost *Basics in Listening – Short Tasks for Listening Development*, page 39; transcript from Teacher's Book, page 100. Lingual House, Tokyo, 1985

6.4.4
Putting pictures in
order

A number of pictures are presented to the students. The aim is to arrange the pictures in the correct order according to the listening text. Generally the ordering can only be done by numbering each picture, because most exercises of this kind are done from books. It is important not to have too many pictures (up to five or six) and to have a series which cannot be put in order easily without listening at all. However, there is no reason why pre-listening work cannot revolve around speculating on the likely order and then if by chance some students get the pictures sorted out before they listen, the actual while-listening stage becomes a matching exercise.

EXAMPLE Part 3

19

TRANSCRIPT

Jenny was out for a walk one day when she came to a gate in a fence. 'I wonder,' she said to herself, 'where this leads to?' She went through it and immediately came face to face with a very fierce-looking dog. It made her nervous.

'Does your dog bite?' she asked the boy who was standing beside the dog. 'No, it doesn't,' he replied. Jenny leaned forward to pat the dog on the head.

'Nice doggie,' she said. But the dog immediately jumped at her and, as she ran for safety towards a tree, it ran after her, growling, and tore a piece of cloth from her coat. 'I thought you said your dog didn't bite,' she said to the boy as she hung from a branch of the tree. 'That's right,' he replied. 'It doesn't. But this isn't my dog.'

From D H Howe and G McArthur *New Access Listening*, page 19; transcript from page 119. Oxford University Press, Hong Kong, 1984

6.4.5
Completing
pictures

This activity is popular with younger students and is particularly useful at the very early stages of learning when the level of difficulty can be kept very low. It is one of a vast range of activities which entail carrying out instructions. Having looked at the basic outline of the picture, the student is required to follow the instructions and draw in (or colour) various items.

It is important for the students to realise that the drawing/colouring is not a test of their artistic skills, but an indication that they have understood. Children often want to 'make a good job' of their drawings, so you might need to tell them to draw just the outlines of the items while they are listening and then they can do the rest later, otherwise the continuity of the listening will be broken.

EXAMPLE

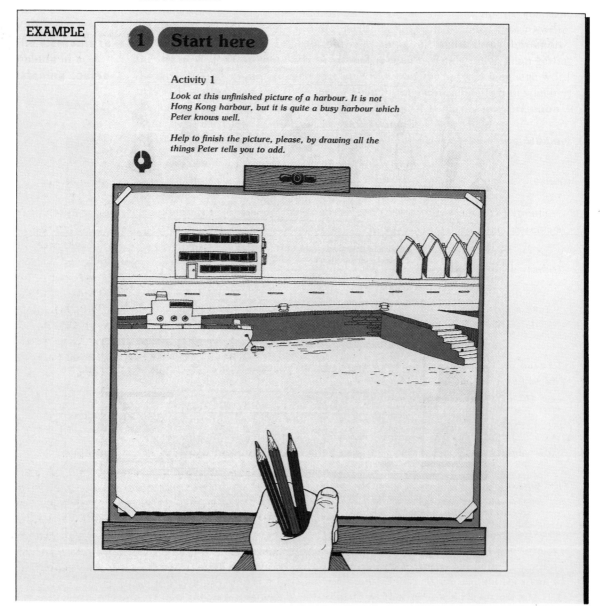

1 Start here

Activity 1

Look at this unfinished picture of a harbour. It is not Hong Kong harbour, but it is quite a busy harbour which Peter knows well.

Help to finish the picture, please, by drawing all the things Peter tells you to add.

TRANSCRIPT

PETER: There are a lot of things to add to the picture. First, there should be one or two more ships.//
And, of course, there are always two or three junks in the water.//
I'd like you to draw a car in the street// and a bicycle, too.//
Oh, look, the tower on top of the big building has been forgotten! Please put a tower at the left-hand end of the big building.//
And I think there should be a flag on top of the tower// – and a clock on the front of it, too.//
Can you put some windows in the small houses on the right of the picture, please?//
I think that's all. Oh no, sorry, I forgot people. There are always lots of people around the harbour. Please draw some people as well.//

From Mary Underwood *Better Listening 2*, page 1; transcript from Teacher's Book, page 6. Oxford University Press, Hong Kong, 1985

6.4.6
Picture drawing

This activity can be done at absolutely any level, at the beginning by asking students to draw simple (known) items – a chair, a tree, a house – and later extending to require advanced students to try to reproduce complicated designs. It is better to use patterns and layouts for advanced work, rather than artistic pictures, as the focus is then on what is required and not on the varying abilities of the students to draw artistically. On some occasions, you can invite the students to work in pairs, one describing the picture and the other attempting to draw it. This has the benefit of giving the students the opportunity to practise turn-taking in listening and speaking and using feedback to elicit the details they need from the speaker. It can, however, lead to frustration if the speaker is unable to convey clear enough messages. One of the 'fun' aspects of having the teacher provide the description is that the students can compare their efforts with others' and then finally see the teacher's own version. A talent for drawing 'stick figures', or at least a willingness to try, is useful here.

6.4.7
Carrying out actions

This kind of activity is generally carried out with young learners at the beginning of their course.

Simply instructing the class to do a series of actions produces good listening practice, and this can be made more motivating by turning it into some sort of game. 'Simon says. . .' is the most popular one. To play, the students must only carry out the instruction when you begin 'Simon says. . .', e.g. 'Simon says "Stand up."' They must do nothing if you simply say 'Stand up.' A variant on this can be for you to say 'Simon says – a car,' 'Simon says – an umbrella,' 'A baby,' and the class must only repeat the item when it is introduced by 'Simon says. . .'. Those who make a mistake and act/speak when they should not do so are 'out' (and can help you watch for others who should be out thereafter).

6.4.8
Making
models/arranging
items in patterns

This is another 'following instructions' activity. Each student (or pair or group of students) is given items with which to build the model or make the pattern. You can then either give the instructions yourself or play them from a tape and the students must try to produce the model/pattern.

For a simple version of the activity, you can provide each student with four or five pencils or different shaped pieces of paper and then give instructions on how they are to be laid out on the students' desks. The same set of items can be used for a number of different patterns and further items can be introduced to add interest after two or three patterns have been made.

For more advanced students, quite sophisticated models can be the basis of the activity. It is, of course, more motivating if the exercise leads to the production of something which students can use and perhaps keep.

EXAMPLE

2 Listen to what the woman says about the first way of making a puppet.
   a) How do you make the *head*? the *hair*? the *eyes*?
   b) Where do you put the cardboard tube? Why?
   c) How is the puppet's dress different from an ordinary doll's dress?
   d) How exactly do you put the puppet on your hand?

3 Listen to what she says about the second way of making a puppet.
   a) Make a list of *all* the materials you need, and what each thing is for.

Material	What it's for
matchbox cover	the puppet's head
paper	

   b) Explain how you put the puppet together on your hand. Begin 'You take the handkerchief, and you put it . . .'

4 Listen to the story about the puppet show she gave in Cornwall.
   a) What kind of puppets did she use?
   b) How did she make her theatre?
   c) How did she find an audience?

Make a matchbox puppet.

TRANSCRIPT

INTERVIEWER: . . . I believe you can also make puppets just using a matchbox and a handkerchief. Is that right?

PUPPETEER: Yes, they're very useful, because they can be made so quickly – you can do them in a few minutes, really. You take a matchbox first to prepare the head, – just the cover of a matchbox – and you stick paper over the coloured label on the matchbox, and on that you can draw a face with felt-tipped pencils. Now when you've done that, you want to put your puppet together. So you take your handkerchief, and put it over your forefinger, spread out your thumb and third finger, and you anchor the whole thing down by putting the matchbox firmly in place on the forefinger, where the head would be. Then you arrange the handkerchief round so that the tips of your puppet's hands are showing at the edge of the handkerchief and you can secure it at the bottom with an elastic band round the wrist if you wish, and then you can use it for quite a while.

INTERVIEWER: So you can make quick puppets. Can you make a quick theatre as well?

PUPPETEER: As a matter of fact, that's just what I did once. I was staying with an artist friend in Cornwall, and she very much wanted to see one of my puppet shows, and I had nothing with me at all. So I made two matchbox puppets, and then, for the theatre I balanced a big gold frame of hers on a chair in a corner of the studio, and draped a sheet over the front. I was all ready to start but I wanted some children, so we both went out into the streets of the village and collected up all the kids we could find, and brought them all in, and we all had a very good time together.

From Adrian Doff, Christopher Jones and Keith Mitchell *Meanings into Words* Intermediate Student's Book, page 27; transcript from Teacher's Book, pages 49–50. Cambridge University Press 1983

6.4.9
Following a route

Following a route on a road plan or a map is a popular and reasonably authentic activity. It is easiest if the map covers a fairly small area, uses road names which are easily recognised and has a small number of features marked on it which will help the listener by confirming that he/she is going the right way, e.g. 'Turn right into Church Road and then go past the station and down to the post office.'

When students have got used to following routes, they can be presented with more complicated maps and routes to follow. As pre-listening work they might be asked to suggest the quickest way from A to B, and then the listening text can tell them which is, in fact, the quickest way.

In addition to using road plans/maps, you can introduce such things as larger scale geographical maps, plans of the school, plans of a hotel, plans of a hospital, etc, which give the opportunity for more listening practice combined with different lexical sets. There are many published exercises of this kind, but you can improvise by finding/drawing a map/plan, marking a chosen route on your own copy and then telling the students the way from A to B so that they too can draw it in. This activity lends itself to the introduction of some local features which make it more relevant to the students.

As well as using these direction-finding activities, you can apply the same principle to such things as scientific diagrams: for example, asking the students to mark the direction of the flow of blood in the body or the passage of information through a computer.

6.4.10
Completing grids[1]

This kind of activity can be used with an enormous range of topics. The teacher provides, or asks students to draw, a grid – i.e. a block of 'boxes' – with each column and row labelled.

Likes:	rice	bananas	chocolate	eggs	fish
Inge					
Hamid					
Anna					
Peter					
Maria					

Students then enter their 'answers' in the correct boxes on the grid, depending on what they discover from the listening text.

If there is a lot of information in the listening text, or the particular group of students might have difficulty in writing it down, you can give some of the answers in advance, either filling them in yourself or providing them at the pre-listening stage.

It is always easier to complete a grid when the information is given in the listening text in the order in which it is needed to fill in the boxes, rather than when it is all jumbled up.

A popular use of grids is for recording information about train or plane times. The activity can be based on recorded material, or you can simply talk about train/plane times and destinations (using a published timetable if one is available).

6.4.11
Form/chart
completion

In addition to the multi-purpose grid (see 6.4.10 above) there is a range of other 'information gap' activities based on forms, charts, etc. In all of these, students are required to take information from the listening text and use it in various kinds of written (or drawn) completion exercises.

This kind of activity proves motivating for most learners, perhaps because it is generally easier to respond to a number of individual stimuli rather than to write down information without a ready-made framework.

Because of the need to keep while-listening activities simple (see 6.2.3 above), it is important to limit what the students are required to write while they are listening. It is often possible to ask them to listen for some answers at the first listening and to leave other parts of the form/chart for subsequent run-throughs. Some published material uses this idea of gradually building up the chart, but in many other cases, where the writer of the material has not suggested this sequencing, it is possible to do the work section-by-section and thus reduce the level of difficulty.

In this example, students are required simply to mark their choices with a cross, and to write very brief answers. It would be possible for students to do the exercise in two parts, during two play-throughs of the listening text.

EXAMPLE

UNIT FOUR
Airport

1 Listen

John is on holiday in London. He goes to a café for a cup of tea, but all the tables are full. John is just going to leave, when a young man stands up. He says, 'You can sit here, I'm just leaving. I'm in a hurry, anyway. I'm going to the airport, and my plane leaves in two hours.'

The young man hurries out, because the café is a long way from the airport.

John sits down and orders a cup of tea. He's just going to stand up and pay his bill, when he sees something between the cushions on the seat. It's a wallet. There's a lot of money in it, but no name.

John telephones the police. Here is part of their conversation.

2 Listen and write

While John is talking, the policeman fills in a form. Can you complete it?

In Part A put a cross (X) in the space beside the words which describe the young man. In Part B fill in the blanks. If you are not sure, put a question mark (?) beside the description you think is correct.

Name _____ Date _____

PART A

Sex male ☐ female ☐

Age child ☐ teenager ☐ young adult ☐ middle-aged ☐ old ☐

Height very short ☐ short ☐ average ☐ tall ☐ very tall ☐

Build thin ☐ slim ☐ medium ☐ well-built ☐ fat ☐

Eyes blue ☐ green ☐ brown ☐ grey ☐

Hair fair ☐ medium ☐ dark ☐ red ☐ grey ☐ white ☐ bald ☐

PART B

Name _____

Nationality _____

Occupation _____

Clothing _____

Luggage _____

Any other important points _____

TRANSCRIPT

POLICEMAN: . . . And where are you now, sir?

JOHN: I'm still in the café. I'm in the manager's office.

POLICEMAN: And you think the wallet belongs to this young man?

JOHN: I'm sure it does. It's got a lot of foreign money in it, I think it's Norwegian. I think the young man comes from Norway. His English is very good, but he speaks with a foreign accent.

POLICEMAN: Well, there are two flights to Norway this afternoon from London. Perhaps we can telephone the airport police and try to find your young man. Can you describe him? Is he tall or short?

JOHN: Tall. Not very tall, but fairly tall.

POLICEMAN: Thin? Fat?

JOHN: Well, he's certainly not fat. He's very fit and strong. But he's not thin either.

POLICEMAN: Can you say he's well-built?

JOHN: Yes, exactly. He's well-built. About twenty-one or twenty-two years old.

POLICEMAN: Fair or dark hair?

JOHN: Oh blond, with a big blond beard.

POLICEMAN: He's got a beard? What about his hair? Is it long or short?

JOHN: About shoulder-length. It's wavy and comes to his shoulders.

POLICEMAN: What colour are his eyes?

JOHN: I don't know. He's got dark glasses.

POLICEMAN: I see. Can you tell us anything else? What's he wearing, for instance?

JOHN: Yes, I can, actually. He's wearing a big white pullover, white shorts and an open-necked shirt.

POLICEMAN: Do you remember the colour of the shirt?

JOHN: No. I don't. It's a checked shirt, blue or green I think. And he's wearing socks and shoes. He's carrying a rucksack and a big waterproof bag. I think he's going home after a camping holiday.

POLICEMAN: No coat?

JOHN: Perhaps he's got one in his rucksack. He isn't wearing one.

POLICEMAN: Can you remember anything else?

JOHN: No. I'm sorry, I can't.

POLICEMAN: Well, thank you for ringing, sir. I'm going to telephone the airport now, and ask them to look for this young man. You stay where you are. There's a policeman on his way to you now.

From Rosemary Aitken *Making Sense*, page 16; transcript from Teacher's Book, pages 25–26. Nelson 1983

6.4.12
Labelling

Quite frequently, in lessons other than English, students label diagrams/pictures to enable them to learn and remember the various parts of a leaf or an engine or whatever. Listening to a short talk/lecture in English and labelling familiar diagrams using English words is a good way of mastering the lexis of a subject with which you are already familiar in your own language. But in addition to this, if the spoken presentation reflects the way lectures on the subject are given in English, then the students also begin to appreciate the format of English lectures. For this reason, this particular activity is useful in the early stages of EAP (English for Academic Purposes) courses.

When the emphasis is not on teaching new lexis, but rather on getting students to listen for expressions of location or direction, then it is possible to provide the labels and simply ask the students to locate them correctly.

In this example, students listen to a fairly formal presentation and are asked to label diagrams as a way of recording the information they hear.

EXAMPLE

📼 Making Notes from a Talk

You will hear a short talk about waste disposal. As you listen, copy and complete the notes and diagrams. (Draw the diagrams in pencil to start with, in rough; you will be able to complete them more neatly later.)

Waste disposal

1   Why are new methods of dealing with waste necessary?
1.1 ...
1.2 ...

2   Where does it come from?

industry 2%

3   Where does it go to?

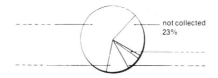

not collected 23%

TRANSCRIPT

Every society produces waste, doesn't it? And that waste has to be disposed of somehow. In fact, societies right throughout history have had the same problem – and the same answer. Stone-Age man collected together his broken pots, his animal bones and his stone chippings, and simply left them in a pile. And today, modern societies do very much the same thing: we collect our waste together, transport it, and dump it (or burn some of it). Yet things *are* beginning to change. We're slowly getting the message that we can't go on indefinitely throwing our waste away – for two reasons. One is that 20th century societies now produce so much waste that it simply doesn't make sense to deal with it in this way. And the other reason is that most waste contains valuable materials that can be extracted and recycled.

Let's firstly talk about where our waste comes from. Basically, there are four sources of waste – it comes from mines, agriculture, industry, and domestic homes. In an average country, waste from mines comprises 39% of the total, and waste from agriculture comprises 53%. Domestic waste accounts for 6%, and industrial waste forms 2%. And where does all this waste go to? Well, most of it goes to open dumps – 55% in fact. 23% is simply not collected and disposed of at all, but is left on the spot. 12% is buried in the ground by the landfill method, and 9% is burnt. That leaves 1%, which is dumped at sea. . . . (ctd)

From Ray Williams *Panorama*, page 22; transcript from Teacher's Book, pages 26–27. Longman 1982

6.4.13
Using lists

A popular while-listening activity consists of making a list, often a shopping list or a list of places to visit. Provided that there is not too much for the students to write and that the information is not given too rapidly, this is a useful activity. However, there are variants on the use of lists which often make better activities.

One of the problems of list-making while listening is that it depends on the students being able to write down the words as well as to recognise them when they hear them. A student who gets stuck with a spelling often concentrates so hard on that word that he/she misses quite a lot of what follows. The skill of not allowing this to happen is one which students need to develop, but in the early stages it is important to avoid the problem and thus avoid the demotivation it can cause. For this reason, it is often better to use lists provided by the teacher/listening book and ask the students to mark the items on the list in some way which indicates that they have (a) heard the words and (b) can match them with the printed words.

It sometimes happens that words on a list are not known to all the students and they will then need to be introduced in pre-listening work (see Chapter 5). However, it *is* possible to ensure that no student is in the position of not knowing a word on the list! To achieve this, the teacher should invite students at the pre-listening stage to make their own lists of what they expect to hear, then make these lists the basis of the while-listening activity. This means that, at the while-listening stage, students will only be matching words which are in their own vocabulary with what they hear and are therefore likely to be much more motivated because of the extent of their success.

At other levels, activities which require the students to annotate or add to lists are suitable, and can be adjusted depending on the level of the group.

Lists can be made up of things, actions, countries, ideas, etc, and can be 'disguised' by being incorporated into questionnaires, forms or charts.

In this example, students have only to insert numbers and can therefore concentrate on continuing to listen; they do not have to struggle with spellings and writing words down.

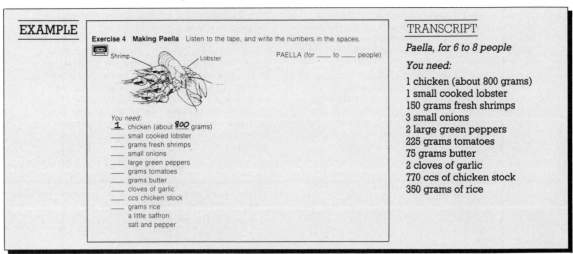

EXAMPLE

Exercise 4   Making Paella   Listen to the tape, and write the numbers in the spaces.

Shrimp   Lobster   PAELLA (for ____ to ____ people)

You need:
__1__ chicken (about **800** grams)
____ small cooked lobster
____ grams fresh shrimps
____ small onions
____ large green peppers
____ grams tomatoes
____ grams butter
____ cloves of garlic
____ ccs chicken stock
____ grams rice
a little saffron
salt and pepper

TRANSCRIPT

Paella, for 6 to 8 people

You need:

1 chicken (about 800 grams)
1 small cooked lobster
150 grams fresh shrimps
3 small onions
2 large green peppers
225 grams tomatoes
75 grams butter
2 cloves of garlic
770 ccs of chicken stock
350 grams of rice

From Steve Elsworth *Count Me In*, page 9; transcript from page 40. Longman 1982

**6.4.14
True/false**

This activity can be used both for listening comprehension and for reading comprehension, but often turns out to be more difficult than anticipated. It is important that true/false exercises are designed in such a way as to avoid the dangers which are described in 6.2.3 above. It is equally important that you check through true/false activities in published materials carefully before using them with classes, noting particularly any where responses can be a matter of opinion/interpretation rather than fact. These can then be the subject of discussion and 'acceptable' responses agreed, rather than some students finding that their answer is not the 'right' one, even though it is a perfectly reasonable choice.

EXAMPLE

Part 1

A *Decide whether the statements about electric cord-extension reels are True or False and tick the appropriate column.*

		T	F
1	They could possibly cause death.		
2	Some tested were made in Hong Kong, some were imported.		
3	All tested were very dangerous.		
4	They should no longer be used in homes.		
5	They are safer than wall sockets.		
6	They are not popular with householders.		
7	A cord-extension reel consists of a socket and a cord, wound round a reel.		
8	They are made by skilled workers.		
9	Their sale in Hong Kong is legal.		

TRANSCRIPT

ANNOUNCER: In Part 1 of this section, you're going to hear a news item about an unsafe electrical product on sale in Hong Kong and used in many homes here. It's called an electric cord-extension reel. Listen to the talk and as you listen, decide whether the statements about electric cord-extension reels in Part 1, A of your Question Book are True or False. Put a tick in the appropriate column.

SPEAKER A: The Consumer Council today issued a warning to all consumers about a potentially dangerous electrical product that is on sale everywhere in Hong Kong. Linda Lee has the story.

SPEAKER B: Would you bring a killer into your home? The answer is, of course, no. However, you may have one there already and be unaware of it, according to the Consumer Council. A spokesman for the Council said today that a device called an electric cord-extension reel, widely available in Hong Kong, could be fatal to users. Although in most cases, he said, the extension reels would give a nasty shock, in some cases they might cause fire or even electrocution.

In response to complaints from angry users, the Council tested eight extension reels, all of them made in Hong Kong and all of them sold locally. They now report that every one of them was a serious threat to the safety of the users. In one of the worst cases, the reel started melting after it had been in normal use for only a few minutes.

The test results are so serious that the Council is calling on owners of such devices to stop using them. A safer alternative, it says, is to have additional wall sockets installed by a qualified electrician. . . . (ctd)

From D H Howe and G McArthur *New Access Listening 4*, page 6; transcript from pages 91–92. Oxford University Press, Hong Kong, 1984

6.4.15
Multiple-choice
questions

Using multiple-choice questions as a while-listening activity can cause the same kinds of problems as those associated with true/false exercises (see 6.2.3 above). However, well-designed multiple-choice questions can help guide students through the text just as ordinary 'open' questions can (see Chapter 5, section 5.8.5.).

If multiple-choice questions are to be answered at the while-listening stage (rather than later), it is often necessary to use a paused tape or to stop the tape to allow the students time to make their choices.

The questions in this example 'guide' the listener through the story. Even though the choices are quite straightforward, it is clear that students need to read through the questions before they listen as it would be extremely difficult to read and listen at the same time.

EXAMPLE

10

Mark the correct answers with a cross (X)

1 *Where do the woman and her children live?*
  a   just outside a town
  b   on a farm in the country
  c   in a small village
  d   in a country town

2 *Why did the woman go to the bank?*
  a   to rob the bank
  b   to take out money from the bank
  c   to put money in the bank
  d   to borrow money from the bank

3 *Where was Mrs Bridges, her babysitter, on this Friday morning?*
  a   at home
  b   in the bank
  c   in town
  d   in the hospital

TRANSCRIPT

The Bank Robbery

I have five small children: two girls and three boys. I don't go out very often because it's difficult for me to find someone to look after them. And any time I want to go out, I have to find a baby-sitter. It's not easy to find a baby-sitter around here: we've moved from the centre of town to the middle of the country, and we now live in a little village about twelve miles from the nearest town.

Well, one Friday morning I looked in my purse and found that I had only one pound left. And I still had to do all the shopping for the weekend! There was just nothing else for it – I had to go to the bank. I hoped that Mrs Bridges, our next-door neighbour, could come in and babysit for me. She's helped me a lot since I came out of hospital. But she wasn't at home. Then I remembered that she always goes to town herself on Fridays, so I helped the children into their clothes and off we went. . . (ctd)

From John McClintock and Borje Stern *Let's Listen* Stage 2, page 20; transcript from page 78. Heinemann Educational Books 1980

6.4.16
Text completion
(gap-filling)

Text completion (gap-filling) is another variety of information transfer exercise. It is generally a harder activity than grid completion as students often have difficulty in keeping up because they are unable to read as quickly as the speaker speaks. Allowing plenty of time at the pre-listening stage for students to go through the text (even guessing at what should be written in the gaps) increases the chances of success. Because of the tendency for students to get left behind, it is advisable to have rather few gaps for completion, and, if a published text has too many, it is a good idea to help the students to complete some before beginning to listen.

Stories, whether true (e.g. news items) or made up (e.g. stories from books) are particularly good for this activity because students are carried along by the story, and the words to be added are often easily decided upon because the context is so apparent.

It is worth ensuring or, in the case of published material, checking that the gaps to be filled provide reasonable and relevant practice. For example, there is little point in requiring students to 'write in' things like unusual street names which they will never need to know in future, or the same word(s) over and over again unless it is something you are anxious they should learn and learn to spell.

Completing lines of poetry or the lines of songs is often fun for students, and pre-listening can be done on making guesses, using the rhyming system or rhythm as clues. If 'original' verses are used, this is one activity where alternative answers are quite acceptable and can give rise to interesting post-listening discussion and even sometimes to amusement (see Example 2).

In Example 1, there are quite a large number of gaps and most students will need to listen more than once to complete the exercise. It is important for the students to have plenty of time to read through the text at the pre-listening stage, particularly with a text of this length.

EXAMPLE 1

Filling In

Listen to the recording, and fill in the blanks. You may listen to the monolog as many times as you need to.

The stewardess had a hectic time on a trip from one coast to the other. Uh, sh—. . .

there were lots of _____ pockets and the plane _____ going up and down
                        1   2

_____ with all the passengers _____ the plane, uh, and trying _____
3   4   5

serve them food and _____, it was just a _____ bad time for her. _____
                     6   7   8

compou-. . . uh, to make matters worse, uh, _____ were lots of passengers
                                            9

_____ were complaining, asking for _____ and glasses of water _____
10   11   12

aspirin and magazines and _____ poor stewardess was just _____ exhausted.
                          13   14

Well, making matters _____ worse, was this kid _____ up and down the
                     15   16

_____ shouting and hitting people _____ making all sorts of _____. And at
17   18   19

one point _____ even, uh, uh, knocked the stewardess _____ into the lap of
          20   21

a, a _____ gentleman. Well, when this _____, she bent down after _____ a
     22   23   24

long, hard trip _____ she smiled sweetly and _____ in the child's ear,
                25   26

"_____ boy, why don't you _____ and play outside?"
 27   28

From Gary James, Charles G Whitley and Sharon Bode *Listening In and Speaking Out* (Intermediate), page 74. Longman, New York, 1980

EXAMPLE 2

Activity 4

A   *This time try to complete the limerick* <u>*before*</u> *you listen to it.*

> There once was a man of Kowloon,
>
> Who decided to go to the moon.
>
> In a bag on his back,
>
> He carried a snack,
>
> And _____ .

B   *Now listen. Which last line do you prefer? Yours or mine?*

C   *Try another one.*

> There was a young man of Lantau,
>
> Who decided to swim to Cheung Chau.
>
> He set off at eight,
>
> So, unless he is late,
>
> He _____ .

D   *Now listen. Whose line do you prefer? Yours or mine?*

From Mary Underwood *Better Listening 2*, page 36. Oxford University Press, Hong Kong, 1985

6.4.17
Spotting mistakes

This activity can be based on a picture, a printed text or simply facts established orally at the pre-listening stage.

If you are in a situation where you depend almost entirely on the coursebook, you can use any clear picture in the book as the focus of the activity. You then talk about the picture, making some deliberate mistakes, and the students are required to indicate each time that they spot a mistake. Unless the work is at a fairly elementary level, it is worth preparing this activity as carefully as you prepare the rest of your lesson so that you avoid 'mistakes' which might not be clear to your students.

'Playing detectives' is popular with most learners. Activities centred round identifying the 'criminal' by the mistakes he/she makes when giving evidence can be devised by teachers or students, and many books include one or two pictures or texts which can be adapted for this purpose.

EXAMPLE

  B   CORRECT THE MISTAKES

Listen to this news report about the Mexican earthquake of September 20th 1985. Then correct the mistakes in Sentences 1–5 and write out the correct sentences in full.

Example The earthquake in Mexico was smaller than the San Francisco earthquake of 1906.

1 First reports say that thousands of people have died.
2 Mexico City, with a population of 15 million, is the world's largest city.
3 The only news coming out of Mexico at the moment is by telephone.
4 The earthquake hit Mexico at 7.19 this evening just as people were getting ready to leave work.
5 It lasted for 15 seconds.

From David Foll, Teresa O'Brien and Kenneth Cripwell *Time for English* Student's Book 3, page 41. Collins 1987

6.4.18
Predicting

Predicting can be used at the pre-listening stage to give students the opportunity to speculate on what they might expect to hear in any given situation (see 5.8.10). As a while-listening activity, predicting is generally a much more precise exercise, concerned with predicting the exact word(s) to be spoken or the kind of response which might be expected. In many cases, there is not one correct prediction and so teachers must be careful not to rule out alternatives which 'fit' perfectly well but which are not, in fact, the words which the speaker actually uses. Indeed, discussion of the alternatives which are supplied by the listeners forms an interesting part of language learning.

It is sometimes possible when using cassettes to stop the recording, by using the 'pause' button, just before the end of an utterance so that the students can attempt to complete it. To do this successfully requires practice, and even then it does not always work satisfactorily. It is generally easier, and therefore more practicable, to stop the tape between speakers and ask the class to forecast the next speaker's words. Clearly, these two different 'stopping points' produce different kinds of prediction practice.

One of the best ways of giving students an opportunity to practise predicting what will be said next is for the teacher, when telling a story or reading a listening text, to pause from time to time for long enough for the students to try to fill the gap. This avoids all the difficulties associated with stopping and re-starting a recorded text, and takes advantage of listeners' natural inclination to complete unfinished utterances. Students quite enjoy this kind of work, particularly when it is done using songs or poems in which the rhymes or rhythms give some clue as to what might follow, and when, rather than writing down their predictions, they are encouraged to speak or sing them aloud in the way that one would naturally fill a gap in someone else's speech.

In the example on pages 70 and 71, a teacher could use **2** as a while-listening 'predicting' activity by stopping the tape after each question, considering the possible answers given by the students, playing the 'correct' answer, and then proceeding to the next question. Students should be able to make reasonable predictions of what Mr Evans will say in answer to the policeman's first two questions by using the information given in the previous activity. For the rest of the answers, students would need to imagine what might have happened, and would no doubt produce a wide variety of possibilities.

e - using Rhyming stories

EXAMPLE

UNIT TEN
It isn't lost, Mr Evans!

1 Listen

Stephen works for an accountancy firm called Evans and Sons. Three hours ago Mr Evans asked Stephen to go to a shop in the town to collect a briefcase. There were important papers in the briefcase. But Stephen didn't come back.

At last he telephones. Mr Evans is very angry. Listen to their conversation.

2 Listen and write

Mr Evans telephones the police. He explains what happened to the briefcase. Here are the questions the policeman asked. What did Mr Evans say?

Policeman:	What's in the briefcase?
Mr Evans:	
Policeman:	Who collected it from the shop?
Mr Evans:	
Policeman:	Where did he go?
Mr Evans:	
Policeman:	Why?
Mr Evans:	
Policeman:	Why did he take the briefcase?
Mr Evans:	
Policeman:	Who picked it up?
Mr Evans:	
Policeman:	Where did she go?
Mr Evans:	
Policeman:	Why?
Mr Evans:	
Policeman:	Why didn't her boss look at it carefully?
Mr Evans:	
Policeman:	Where did he take it?
Mr Evans:	
Policeman:	Where is it now?
Mr Evans:	

TRANSCRIPT

2

POLICEMAN: What's in the briefcase?
MR EVANS: **Important papers.**
POLICEMAN: Who collected it from the shop?
MR EVANS: **Stephen.**
POLICEMAN: Where did he go?
MR EVANS: **To the petrol station.**
POLICEMAN: Why?
MR EVANS: **He needed some petrol.**
POLICEMAN: Why did he take the briefcase?
MR EVANS: **It was very important.**
POLICEMAN: Who picked it up?
MR EVANS: **A woman.**

POLICEMAN: Where did she go?
MR EVANS: **London.**
POLICEMAN: Why?
MR EVANS: **She thought it was her boss's briefcase.**
POLICEMAN: Why didn't her boss look at it carefully?
MR EVANS: **He was in a hurry.**
POLICEMAN: Where did he take it?
MR EVANS: **To the airport.**
POLICEMAN: Where is it now?
MR EVANS: **Halfway to Rio de Janeiro.**

From Rosemary Aitken *Making Sense*, pages 40–41; transcript from Teacher's Book, pages 54–55. Nelson 1983

6.4.19
Seeking specific
items of
information

Almost all while-listening activities require students to seek bits of information, but this particular activity is concerned with listening to a fairly extensive listening text (a weather forecast, a news bulletin, a discussion, etc) with the objective of finding some previously specified information. The activity is made more motivating when 'real' listening texts are used and the students are asked to find information which is needed for a particular, real, purpose. For example, the students might be asked to listen to the BBC World Service news and find the latest information on an international sports event to put on the English language notice board.

There are lots of exercises of this type in published English teaching material, where students are asked to find the answers to series of questions by listening to a range of recorded texts.

The important aspect of this type of activity is the need for the students to seek out specific items and to let the other parts pass. It gives them practice in 'pricking up their ears' at points when they think the information they want is about to be given.

EXAMPLE

6 [oo] Listening

Listen to this person talking about a burglary at his house. Note down as you listen:

What was taken:
What damage was done:
How the burglar broke in:
What he did about it:

TRANSCRIPT

Well, I came back at about seven thirty in the evening, opened the door, sat down, made myself a cup of tea and the other person in the flat came in. He went upstairs. And I hadn't noticed anything peculiar, saw someone's door was open and thought that they had come back early and gone out again. And my friend then shouted down 'We've been burgled'. So that was the first thing I knew about it. I then obviously went straight upstairs to see what had happened, and found the room totally devastated, papers all over the place and the whole of the house was in that state as well. It was most, it was distressing to think that your own private life had been in someways destroyed and that someone had been in your house, been looking through all your private papers, been taking down addresses maybe and taking your stuff and. . .

What sort of things did they take?

I lost a stereo tape deck, a stereo record deck, another friend lost a digital watch, and apart from that a suitcase as well which obviously the criminal took the things away in.

So presumably the most distressing thing was not what you'd lost but the damage they'd done?

Well, they hadn't actually done any physical damage, but they'd left the place in a considerable mess. They'd turned over all of the rooms. Luckily we didn't have any locks on doors or locks on drawers and things like that, so the person didn't actually have to break into things.

How did they actually break into the house?

Well, we believe that the person must have forced the front door.

So what did you do? What action did you take when you discovered you'd been robbed?

Well, the first thing was to ring the police up, and they were very prompt. A policeman came round in about five minutes. Other than that, try and find out what had been taken, contact the neighbours and see whether anyone had heard anything or seen anything unusual.

From Brian Abbs and Ingrid Freebairn *Studying Strategies* Student's Book, page 20; transcript from Teacher's Book, page 12. Longman 1982

6.5
The importance of immediate feedback

Whatever activities you choose to use, it is important to provide immediate feedback on whether, and to what extent, the students have succeeded in the task(s), and why or why not. It is extremely difficult to provide useful feedback at a later lesson, as it is generally necessary to replay, or respeak, the listening text in order to refer to the salient points, and it is very hard to rekindle interest in a 'past' topic or text. In addition, much of the value of discussing why students have missed things or made errors is lost if the discussion is not held immediately, while relevant thoughts are uppermost in everyone's mind.

Frequently, pair or group checking can follow while-listening activities and can lead to interesting post-listening consideration of the text and the task(s).

6.6
Teacher talk

There are many occasions in class when listening occurs and the listeners' attention is held without the need for any kind of while-listening activities. This kind of listening practice is invaluable because it is the most natural form of listening and provides opportunities for natural responses.

In recent years, teachers have been exhorted to talk less in class and allow students more time to talk. However, it is important, particularly in countries where little English is heard outside the classroom, that this does not lead to teachers failing to talk to their classes in English sufficiently for them to get accustomed to hearing the naturally spoken language which they are learning to understand and use.

Discussion

1 How can while-listening activities be made more motivating for the students you teach? Which of the activities in this chapter are likely to succeed with your students?
2 To what extent do you think while-listening work should be done by each individual student working alone (even if post-listening work is a 'joint' effort)?

Exercises

1 Examine the listening work provided in the coursebook you use, or in any coursebook you know well, and decide whether it provides a sufficient range of while-listening activities for your students. If it does not do so, can you supplement it in any way?
2 Look at two or three examples of published while-listening exercises and find ways to make each one easier for the learner.
3 Think of a story you know (true or otherwise) and produce a while-listening activity which one of your classes would enjoy. Then, of course, try it out!

References

1 A number of interesting ideas for using grids can be found in P Ur 1984 *Teaching Listening Comprehension*. Cambridge University Press

7

The post-listening stage

Post-listening activities embrace all the work related to a particular listening text (whether recorded or spoken by the teacher) which are done after the listening is completed. Some post-listening activities are extensions of the work done at the pre-listening and while-listening stages and some relate only loosely to the listening text itself.

The most common form of post-listening activity has, in the past, been the answering of multiple-choice questions or 'open' questions based on a spoken text (often, in fact, a piece of prose which was meant to be read silently, not to be spoken aloud). For many years, this type of exercise was almost the only kind of listening work done, probably as a result of the type of questions used in public examinations when listening tests were first introduced. Many listening tests are still based on this format, and so it is important for students who have to take these tests to practise answering these kinds of questions. It is, however, quite a difficult activity and depends not only on listening ability but also on reading skills (to read and understand the questions), writing skills (to write down the answers to the questions) and memory (to remember what was said for long enough to be able to produce the answers). To add to the difficulty, the questions are often written in such a way that they do not 'match' the language of the listening text and so the listener has to sort out both the information and the language in order to produce the answers.

If one of the students' objectives is to pass an examination which includes this type of question, then one of the purposes of post-listening work must be to practise for the exam. But there are other purposes for post-listening work which are of wider relevance and apply to all learners, and which teachers of groups at all levels, not just examination classes, should consider.

One of these is checking whether the students have understood what they needed to understand and whether they have completed whatever while-listening task has been set successfully. This can be done by the teacher giving the answers orally, by pairs checking each other's answers, by the teacher showing the answer on the overhead projector/blackboard, by group discussion, by asking the students to check against answers given in a book, and so on. It is best done immediately and without paying too much attention to precisely how many answers individual students have got 'right' or 'wrong'. While-listening activities should not generally be used for giving marks as this discourages students from making guesses (which is part of how we all listen in everyday life and should be encouraged).

Another purpose of post-listening work is to reflect on *why* some students have failed to understand or missed parts of the message. Discussion often occurs at the checking stage and the teacher then has the opportunity to draw attention to specific parts of the listening text and focus on the forms, functions, lexis, stress and intonation which have caused problems for the listeners. However, since one of the skills of listening is being able to 'tolerate vagueness' (see page 18) it is *not* a good idea to go through the listening text explaining word by word at the post-listening stage any more than at the pre-listening stage. Attention should be limited to the points which were significant in achieving the aim of completing the task and those which the students themselves raise because they want to know more about them. Having identified a particular point for attention, you can often take the opportunity to expand on it a little and give a 'mini lesson' on the particular feature of the language. If it is a feature that occurs more than once in the listening text, the passage can be replayed to show the students further examples in a now familiar context. Some published listening materials identify features which recur or which the authors think are worthy of extra attention, but it is, of course, for the teacher to decide, in the light of the group's performance and previous knowledge, which features to focus on at the post-listening stage.

The following example presents language and stylistic points for the students to be made aware of at the post-listening stage. After listening to a conversation about the Chinese lion dance, the students are asked to note the points in the 'Commentary' section.

EXAMPLE

(A group of acrobats from the People's Republic of China recently visited London. Now we hear Angela Huth, Dr Endymion Wilkinson and Nick Stewart talking about the most spectacular item on their programme.)

Huth   I would like to think that most people would probably pick out as the most impressive act the lion act – where they're dressed up as lions. Can you explain the tradition of this – why did – how did this come about?

Wilkinson Well, I think in China itself you no longer see it, but the lion dance was part of festivals, especially in South

China, and many people may have seen it in London – in Gerrard Street – they've revived this, the lion dance; but here was this extraordinary sight of two people in a lion's costume jumping onto a ball, balancing the ball up a seesaw, and rolling down on the other side with all the feet in harmony.

Huth And not being able to see?

Wilkinson I don't know if they could see; I'm sure there must have been visors through the –

Stewart I'm sure they must have been able to see; it was most incredible, the way they stepped around on top of those poles, crossed their legs and balanced. Fantastic. I think they must have been able to see, or else –

Huth Do you think – the head of the troupe said he thought that was probably the most difficult of all their acts. Would you agree with that, Nick?

Stewart Yes, I would, most definitely. It was a great combination of dexterity of footwork between two people enclosed in what I should imagine was a very heavy costume . . .

Huth Now has that act been westernised at all or is it just as they perform in China?

Wilkinson I think the only sign of westernisation would be that the mask of the lion was extremely – mechanical –

Stewart Yes, it lacked the real devilry of the Chinese –

Wilkinson It was smiling rather than grimacing.

Stewart A benevolent lion.

Huth Yes – that's a sign of their humour again, isn't it? . . .

Wilkinson Yes, yes. . . .

Commentary

1   None of the three speakers sounds very relaxed or confident, and none expresses himself easily, except perhaps Nick Stewart. Angela Huth, the interviewer, is anxious not to seem too positive or dogmatic – it is her job to ask questions, not provide the answers.

2   She uses 'would' to indicate 'probability' – 'I would think that most people would probably pick out the lion act . . .' '. . . would you agree with that?' When she has to explain something, she rushes through the

explanation at great speed (perhaps because she does not want to sound boring) and even rushes into the next sentence before she stops for an instant to mark the end of her long word-group:

VERY FAST . . . . ➤

. . . / the *lion* act / where they're dressed up as lions can you explain / the tradition of this / . . .

However, the beginning of the new sentence is marked quite clearly by a very sudden and sharp rise of the voice on *CAN you explain* . . .

3   Dr Wilkinson speaks with some hesitation and also uses expressions which make him sound less positive: '*I think* you no longer see it . . . many people *may* have seen it . . .' He is happier when he has turned the conversation back to a description of the dance: 'but here was this extraordinary sight . . .'

4   Nick Stewart, by contrast, is much more confident and assertive and uses expressions like 'I'm sure they must have been able to see . . .' 'Yes, I would (agree), most definitely . . .'

At the end of the interview, the three speakers all join happily in the game of trying to find the right word to describe the lion's mask; here, the conversation becomes almost 'operatic', with each voice coming in over the top of the voice before it. This is the only part of the interview which sounds like a natural conversation between three people.

From Roger Owen *People Talking*, pages 35–37. BBC 1976

A third purpose is to give students the opportunity to consider the attitude and manner of the speakers of the listening text. People listening to their native language generally recognise the attitude of speakers as they are speaking, but it is sometimes more difficult when listening to a foreign language. At the post-listening stage, students can consider the attitudes of the speakers and what it is that has conveyed those attitudes. Not all listening texts provide the opportunity for this kind of activity, and there is a vast range of different ways in which speakers show their attitudes, but it is a useful activity and one which is enjoyed, particularly for students who can deal with authentic listening texts.

Another purpose of post-listening work is to expand on the topic or language of the listening text, and perhaps transfer things learned to another context. Indeed, many activities which purport to be post-listening activities are of this type. They are not, strictly speaking, listening activities at all. They are activities which can be linked to listening and are more general language learning activities. This does not mean that they should not be done, but it should be recognised that they do not give practice in listening skills, although the additional language learning might well enable students to listen more successfully on future occasions.

Here, having listened to a discussion and having completed a variety of pre- and while-listening work, students are asked to consider whether they agree with the decision taken by the speakers and to express their own views.

EXAMPLE

Now listen to
TAPE

A/B
Conclusion

This is Catherine talking about what she and Tom decided to do. Do you think it's a good solution?

ON YOUR OWN

Why do some couples get along easily and others don't?

What kind of person do you get along with most easily? Why?

From Michael Rost and John Lance *PAIRallels*, pages 38–39. Lingual House, Tokyo, 1984

Finally, some activities which are done after the students have listened to a text are not really post-listening activities because they are, in fact, themselves the main purpose of the lesson and the listening is no more than an introduction or stimulus for the planned work. This does not invalidate the listening stage, but it does mean that teachers have to choose input which is easily handled by the group, otherwise the listening activity takes up too much time and effort and detracts from the main activity.

7.2
The nature of post-listening work

Post-listening activities can be much longer than while-listening activities because at this stage the students have time to think, to discuss, to write. Activities which go further than merely checking comprehension need to have a purpose of their own. If the pre-listening stage has built up expectations in the listeners, and the while-listening stage has satisfied these expectations, it is hard to sustain interest at the post-listening stage unless the post-listening activity is intrinsically motivating. For this reason, you need to find something more interesting than comprehension questions and 'Find the word which means . . .' exercises for your students to do.

7.2.1
Problem-solving and decision-making

Problem-solving and decision-making are popular post-listening activities and follow naturally from many while-listening activities. To maintain interest, it is important not to have exceedingly long and complicated problems to solve, nor decisions where too many factors need to be taken into account (see 7.4.7 below).

Newspaper stories can be read by the teacher and used for problem-solving activities. It is important to prepare for this kind of activity and to make sure that everyone knows what the problem to be solved is. If the group might find it hard to remember the story, a while-listening chart-filling exercise can be used so that everyone has a 'summary' to refer to at the post-listening stage. In addition, any bits of the story which the students may want to hear again should be repeated.

There are lots of examples of problem-solving/decision-making exercises in published materials, but one of the most motivating activities is trying to solve problems which either you or one of the students has in real life. (Everyone likes to solve other people's problems!) You might, for example, say:

'I've got a problem. An old aunt of mine, who lives a long way away, gave me her piano three years ago. When it arrived at my flat, I realised that it was a very poor piano, not nearly as good as the old one I already had. Auntie thought her piano was wonderful, of course. Anyway, I decided not to keep her piano and I sold it. I didn't tell her what I'd done because I thought it would upset her. When she asked "How's the piano?" I always said "Oh, fine!" or "It's wonderful!" Now she's coming to visit me! Another aunt of mine is bringing her to my flat next Saturday. I never dreamed that she would ever come to my place. What *am* I to do?'

7.2.2 Interpreting

Sometimes the actual *words* one hears do not convey the meaning intended by the speaker. For example, 'Yes' spoken in a very doubtful, hesitant manner may mean 'No'. At a more general level, it is often possible to obtain more message than that conveyed by the words spoken. Whilst much of this is gleaned by the listener at the while-listening stage, there is often scope for further exploration afterwards. Authentic material is particularly useful for this kind of work, when students can be asked to decide, for example, what is going on and where the speakers are, even when much of the meaning of the actual words is beyond them. And trying to establish the relationships between speakers in authentic situations gives valuable practice in identifying some of the many ways in which various language functions are carried out.

If you want to plan for this kind of activity, it is essential to listen to the actual recording (not just read the transcript) in order to identify such things as mood, attitudes or relationships and to determine what it is that conveys these to the listener.

7.2.3 Role-play

Basing role-play on listening provides students with at least some language which they can use when their turn comes to speak. Many teachers use listening texts to demonstrate to students how speakers of English behave in a situation and then ask the students, in pairs or in groups, to play the various roles. Frequently, attention is focussed on imitating the situation and the students begin the role-play immediately. More value can be derived from the listening part of the activity if, before the role-play, attention is focussed on the functions and forms which were used by the speakers. This encourages the students to try out some newly heard language rather than simply using language they have already mastered in some other context.

7.2.4 Written work

Post-listening written work can take many forms, from listing specific points to writing summaries or even essays. To link extensive writing exercises with a listening text, it is advisable to have some discussion in class about the topic which is to be written about. For example, a written summary of a story is likely to be more successful if some oral summarising has been done first.

To make post-listening written work more meaningful, it is sometimes possible to 'overlap' it with a while-listening activity. The while-listening task gives a pattern for the activity and then the post-listening part is a kind of extension of that pattern.

EXAMPLE

Michael and Mary discuss what he might have found in the envelope. Find that part of the story on the tape (about half way through) and list the four possibilities mentioned. Then add five more possibilities of things which you think he could have found.

TRANSCRIPT

MICHAEL: Well . . . I, for two or three days afterwards I kept getting it out and looking at it and thinking [Yes] 'Shall I open it?' or 'Shall I try and find out how to open it?' Well, I put it in a cigar box and covered it with cotton wool because just, just handling it made little bits fall off of it. And, er, we had no idea what was in (here). I mean the fact that it was sealed and the fact that it said 'A Prize for You' on the envelope gave us all sorts of ideas. [Yes] We thought we'd got the deeds to the rest of the street or . . .

MARY: Thousands of pounds!

MICHAEL: Thousands of pounds, yes, or a treasure map, you know–five paces north from the pear tree. [laughter] Or, favourite was, er, the bill for mending the roof in 1851. [laughter]

From Mary Underwood *What a Story!* page 113; transcript from page 198. Oxford University Press 1976

7.3
Factors which affect the choice of post-listening activities

In selecting post-listening activities, attention should be given to the following factors (in addition to the general factors listed in 5.6):

(a) how much language work you wish to do in relation to the particular listening text;

(b) whether there will be time to do much post-listening work at the end of the listening lesson (if that is how your timetable is organised);

(c) whether the post-listening work should consist of speaking, reading or writing;

(d) whether the post-listening stage is seen as an opportunity for pair/groupwork or whether it is intended that students should work alone;

(e) whether it is necessary to provide post-listening activities which can be done outside the classroom (at home/in the listening centre);

(f) how motivating the chosen activity will be and whether it can be made more motivating;

(g) whether the listening text lends itself to post-listening work at all, or whether the 'lack of momentum' at the end of the while-listening stage would make post-listening an anti-climax and, therefore, not motivating.

7.4
Ideas for post-listening activities

This section offers a selection of ideas for post-listening work, with examples taken from various published sources. As in the case of the pre-listening and while-listening selections in Chapters 5 and 6, the examples come from materials designed for a range of levels, but the basic idea of each activity can be adapted for use with other texts at other levels.

Some activities seem to 'straddle' the two stages of while- and post-listening, and their being placed in one group rather than the other is determined only by the length and complexity of the task to be completed. Simple tasks can be done while-listening; more complex ones, and those which require more writing, have to be done at the post-listening stage.

**7.4.1
Form/chart
completion**

Form/chart completion tasks which can be carried out while listening are dealt with in 6.4.11, but there are occasions on which the completion of some sections can only be done at a more leisurely pace after listening. Because the recording of factual information after listening depends largely upon memory rather than on listening skills, it is best if post-listening chart completion does not depend on large quantities of information from the listening text. Indeed, a chart can have a section which provides a post-listening opportunity for the students to respond to, or react to, something noted in earlier sections at the while-listening stage (as in the example below).

EXAMPLE

2.2 Now complete the following table. If you don't remember, listen again to this first part of the students' discussion. Afterwards report to the class.

Does Chris state/imply any of the following reasons for including a diagram of a food-cycle in a brochure?	And what do you think? (short notes)
a People may get interested in the problem of pollution when they see how nicely balanced nature is when you leave it alone. yes ☐ no ☐	
b Visual material always attracts people's attention. ☐ ☐	
c People will realize that this is the way nature works in their own area and will therefore identify with it, in other words, see it as something belonging to them. ☐ ☐	
d It's necessary to point out to people that there is a balance in nature before you can explain to them how not to destroy it or how to restore it. ☐ ☐	

From Françoise Grellet, Alan Maley and Wim Welsing *Quartet* Student's Book 2, page 68. Oxford University Press 1983

7.4.2
Extending lists

This activity can 'straddle' the while-listening and post-listening stages. The students are asked to make a list or tick/check a list while listening, and then to add to it after the listening is finished. It provides a way of collecting word sets and/or extending word sets already known to the students.

EXAMPLE

6.3   Susan asks for advice about getting a temporary job.

As a full-time student, Susan finds that she has time to get a job, to earn a little money, during the Christmas vacation. She is not sure about how to find a job for such a short time and she asks Felix and Scilla for advice.

. . . .
Exercise 2

List all the jobs mentioned by Felix and Scilla as they try to advise Susan. You should find six. Add to your list six other jobs which Susan might be able to do on a temporary basis.

From Mary Underwood *Have You Heard . . .?* pages 52–53. Oxford University Press 1979

7.4.3
Sequencing/
'grading'

The difficulties of doing sequencing activities at the while-listening stage are discussed in 6.2.3. At the post-listening stage they are much more likely to succeed, especially if the students have the opportunity to replay the recording if they wish to check something. What tends to happen is that the students attempt to sort out the various items as they listen and then to complete the activity after they have heard the whole passage/story. A list of more than about seven or eight items is difficult and frustrating to handle as the students have to make lots of alterations to their ordering.

Stories are the easiest texts to use for ordering as the students are helped by the natural development of the story as it unfolds. If you plan to produce the items to be sorted, you must take care not to have a list which can be sorted without listening to the text at all, as the exercise then becomes something other than listening practice. On the other hand, it does not matter if one or two of the items have an obvious position in the sequence, and, in fact, it can be positively helpful to less able students who will then have at least some success.

Activities which require some kind of 'grading' rather than sequencing tend to be more difficult. For example, students may be asked to 'put in order, from the most liked to the least liked' six jobs that the speaker has to do. This will require more detailed listening than sequencing events in a story (unless the speaker delivers the facts as a straightforward checklist).

7.4.4
Matching with a
reading text

This activity is particularly useful for students who have so far learned their English mainly through reading and writing and who have difficulty in matching the heard word with the written word. At first, it is probably best to start from the written word and use reading as the pre-listening activity.

However, when the students have had more practice in listening and their confidence has begun to build up, it is a good idea to ask them to listen, and carry out a while-listening task, before referring them to a reading text on the same topic. The obvious source of material for this is the news, from radio and from newspapers, but you can improvise by taking a printed news item and then recounting its content to the class before showing the students the printed version.

The best exercises are those which do not simply ask the students to match words or phrases from the two texts (the listening text and the reading text), but require the students to listen carefully for information needed to complete a task which depends on successful matching.

In the example below, students match people to actions.

EXAMPLE

Now listen to
TAPE

[A]

Ethel Hillman is explaining a plan of action to Murray Gavin and Spider MacDonald.

After you listen...

Put the actions next to the name of the person who will perform them.

a. cross the ledge

b. go down the fire stairs (fire escape)

c. unlock the main doors

d. cut the glass

e. open the metal shutters

f. wait at the corner of 12th Street and Wendell

g. shut off the alarm system

h. take the canvas bag

i. put everything in the briefcase

j. wait and follow two minutes later

k. go to the east stairs

l. signal two times

Benny	
Ethel	
Spider	
Murray	

From Michael Rost and John Lance *PAIRallels*, page 51. Lingual House, Tokyo, 1984

7.4.5
Extending notes
into written
responses

Brief notes made at the while-listening stage can be extended into written texts, although taking notes while listening is a difficult activity and can only be done by students at a fairly advanced level. The written text which is required can be anything from one-sentence answers to specific questions to long pieces of prose. It is a good idea for the students to listen again after the post-listening writing stage to check their work, as this helps them to make connections between how the language looks and how it sounds.

In this particular example, students are required to use the notes they take while listening to a speaker at a seminar on 'Development and aid' to carry out post-listening written work. It is an activity which can be applied to a wide range of spoken presentations.

EXAMPLE

LISTENING ACTIVITY
Listen to the recording. Make notes on the extract. Remember – try to be as *selective*, *brief* and *clear* as possible.

Notes:

POST-LISTENING ACTIVITY
First, compare your notes with someone else's. Have you left out anything important?

Then, summarise the extract from your notes. What is the general point made by the speaker?

Do you agree with his point? Can you suggest further examples to make the same point? Or can you present *counter-examples* that disprove it?

TRANSCRIPT

and finally / in this brief introduction I want to look at the area of technological innovation and industrial development / um / in a lot of the discussion of development which you can read / there seems to be a general assumption that development is a sort of race / the industrialised countries are ahead / and the developing countries are in the same race / they're just further behind and they are going to follow the same path / there's the assumption that the pattern of development they follow has to be the same or at least very similar / to the one that the industrialised countries have already gone through /

for example / you'll find that er all over the third world there are hospitals being built which are basically the same as hospitals in the industrialised countries / they produce they use the same form of high medical technology to treat patients coming in / whereas in fact what the patients are suffering from are the so-called diseases of poverty / er undernourishment and the various diseases produced by bad hygiene and so on / in other words they're used as curative hospitals / whereas what's really needed are education programmes and preventive medicine / or if you turn to the example of farming . . . (ctd)

From Tony Lynch *Study Listening*, pages 23–24; transcript from pages 91–92. Cambridge University Press 1983

7.4.6
Summarising

Summarising can be done by extending notes made at the while-listening stage (see 7.4.5 above) or by simply depending on memory. If students are to depend on memory, it is generally best to use a story as the listening text, as the sequence of a story, and, one hopes, the interest, make remembering easier.

Asking students to write summaries generates a lot of marking, so you should only use this activity if you are prepared to do the marking! It is, of course, possible to do oral summary work, perhaps by getting pairs/small groups to go through the story and make notes and then asking one or two people to retell the story whilst the rest of the class listens for any errors or omissions.

EXAMPLE

5. [cassette] LISTENING. A newspaper reporter is interviewing people on the street on New Year's Eve to get information for an article he's writing. Listen to the interviews and write the information in the reporter's notebook.

From Francisco Lozano and Jane Sturtevant *Life Styles* Student's Book 1, page 91. Longman, New York, 1981

7.4.7
Using information from the listening text for problem-solving and decision-making activities

Students can be asked to collect information from a listening text, or from a listening text and other sources as well (e.g. a reading text/pictures/a chart), and apply the information to the solution of a problem or as the basis for a decision. If the problems are difficult to solve or the decisions difficult to reach, the students get more practice in reasoning, and in defending/attacking ideas. However, if the primary purpose is to encourage careful listening, then the focus should be on the elicitation of the necessary information from the text to solve simpler problems or reach less difficult decisions. Again, a while-listening activity can be used to discover the information and the interpretation and application can be done at the post-listening stage. In published material, this kind of activity is usually the culmination of a series of activities based on a particular listening text, and the students are generally required to discuss, in pairs/groups, and come up with an answer, or to write something (a paragraph/a letter) in which they give their answers/opinions, as in **2** in the example below.

EXAMPLE

Listening comprehension

You will hear interviews with three people. The first time you hear them, try to identify the situation: who are these people? Why and by whom are they being interviewed? Then listen again, and answer questions 1 to 3.

1 Fill in the missing information about the objects described by the interviewees. Write as briefly as possible.

2 Write a brief newspaper report (100–150 words) on the phenomenon which the interviewees claim to have witnessed. Give your opinion, with reasons, on the truth of their statements.

3 What were the exact words used to
   a ask for information?
   b express certainty and uncertainty?
   c express lack of knowledge?

	man	woman	child
shape			
colour			
size			
movements			
sounds			
surface texture			

TRANSCRIPT

THE SENSES

INTERVIEWER: Mr Davies, thank you for coming along. I'd like to ask you some questions about the phenomenon you observed last night.

MR DAVIES: Sure. Well, it probably sounds a bit odd, but it looked like a big white banana, with small red lights on. It flew across the sky at a tremendous speed, completely, er, soundless.

INTERVIEWER: What time was this?

MR DAVIES: About two in the morning, so it was pitch black. I think it must have been about a couple of hundred feet above the ground, and I should say it was about twenty feet long and three or four feet across. It seemed to have a dull, metallic surface.

INTERVIEWER: Do you have an explanation, Mr Davies? What do you think it was?

MR DAVIES: Haven't a clue. I've never seen anything like it before.

INTERVIEWER: Well, thank you very much, Mr Davies. Mrs Evans, then. I wonder if you could tell me exactly what happened last night.

MRS EVANS: Well, I was woken up by a sort of low murmuring noise . . . (ctd)

From Michael Hinton and Robert Marsden *Options*, page 82; transcript from pages 209–210. Nelson 1985

7.4.8
Jigsaw listening

'Jigsaw listening' is a term which was used by Marion Geddes and Gill Sturtridge in the late 1970s[1] to describe a listening activity in which a class of students is divided into a small number of groups and each group listens to a different listening text, although all the texts are on the same topic, and then the groups exchange information to build up the complete picture. The success of a jigsaw activity depends on each listening text being incomplete in some way which is crucial for the completion of the task, so that the students need to seek details from each other and provide accurate information from their own listening. When there is quite a lot of information contained in the listening texts, it is useful to provide a while-listening activity which requires the students to record, on a chart for example, points which they may need to convey to the other groups at the post-listening stage.

A good topic for jigsaw work is the story of a crime told by two or three different witnesses. Each group is given the evidence of just one witness, and then everybody, from all of the groups, has to try to work out who committed the crime. To do this, the students have to share the information they have received from their various witnesses. In fact, many sets of listening texts which give two or three views of the same situation or incident can make satisfactory material for this kind of exercise, e.g. reports of an argument given, say, by the two people involved and someone who overhead it, or the views of a mother and father and their child on the child coming home later than agreed.

It is important to note that, whilst jigsaw listening can be very motivating and enjoyable, to make it run smoothly it has to be very well planned. Unless you are sure that you have (a) good material, (b) the facilities and space for each of your groups to listen to the texts undisturbed by the other groups, and (c) the organisational skills to manage the class so that the whole thing runs smoothly, you should not launch straight into jigsaw listening activities. It would be better, first, to try some jigsaw *reading* work, so that your students get used to the pattern of the activity, and then, if and when you feel you can handle the additional complications of using listening texts, try jigsaw listening.

7.4.9
Identifying relationships between speakers

Although listeners can often identify the relationships between speakers while they are actually listening to them, it is sometimes useful, at the post-listening stage, to consider what features of the listening text made the relationships clear. In some cases, the lexis is sufficient (e.g. the forms of address, references to shared knowledge); in others the features are more subtle. By discussion of these features, the students' awareness of how language is used in particular social settings will be raised and they will gradually appreciate how far, and in what ways, English differs from their own languages in this respect.

For this type of practice, authentic material is by far the best, although something can be achieved with really well-produced non-authentic material.

If you intend to hold a post-listening discussion about relationships, you can give the students notice by giving a question or two *before* listening, so that they will focus on this aspect while they are listening.

EXAMPLE

This is a conversation between two unusual speakers. Who are they? Where does this conversation take place?

TRANSCRIPT

A: Request permission to enter.
B: Come in. Come in. Could I have your report please?
A: A routine mission. Nothing to write home about. We made a standard 30,000 light year visit to a neighbouring galaxy and brought back life samples for analysis.
B: Hmm. What was the place like?
A: Oh, a nice place. Nice colours, greens and blues. Some interesting features.
B: Any system of interaction?
A: I suppose you could say so. It's a rather primitive system, predominantly physical – physical objects moving around on two dimensional planes, boxes moving on rails, things like that.
B: How about the life samples?
A: I kind of like them. They have very soft surfaces, quite sensitive, very nice to touch actually.
B: Did your approach hurt them?
A: I'm afraid I did shock them a little. I really did try to come in as gently as I could, but . . .
B: Did you go into a physical mode?
A: Yes. I thought that would be the best way to communicate . . . so I selected a mode of light and a type of vibration that I hoped would be pleasing

to them, but maybe I came on a little too strong.
B: Mmm. Yes, that happens sometimes. Don't let it worry you too much. Bring back anything besides the samples?
A: Yes, um, I brought back two souvenirs . . . I was hoping you might let me keep them . . . take them back home. One is this thing, it makes a sort of noise . . . (music)
B: What is that noise?
A: Don't know, really. Haven't been able to analyze it yet. And the other is this sort of visual record . . . they call it a 'magazine'.
B: Then you must have analyzed their language through this from this magazine?
A: That's right, yes.
B: And you programmed this language into me before you came in.
A: Yes, I did. I hope you like it.
B: It is rather enjoyable. What do they call it?
A: English.
B: Hmm. Interesting. Now, how about the samples? Could you bring them in please?
A: Oh, certainly . . . (OK, would you two mind coming in here for a minute . . .?)

From Michael Rost and John Lance *PAIRallels*, page 28; transcript from Teacher's Book, page 22. Lingual House, Tokyo, 1984

7.4.10
Establishing the
mood/attitude/
behaviour of the
speaker

This activity is similar to the one above in that it depends on the listener interpreting what is said, rather than just looking for the overt meaning. It is not just the words that are important but how they are spoken. A comment such as 'You're so kind' can be spoken with varying stress and intonation to show that the words are spoken sincerely/sarcastically/fawningly/etc. The loudness/quietness of a voice might indicate anger or sorrow, excitement or boredom. Variations in delivery often have the same significance across many languages, or groups of languages, but this is certainly not always so, and the types of misunderstanding which can occur through non-recognition of the underlying meaning, as opposed to the surface meaning of the words spoken, can be significant.

As students' command of the language increases and their listening confidence develops, their perception of meanings which may be hidden behind words can be heightened by post-listening discussion of what was actually meant and how the listener can know this.

Again, authentic material is best for this kind of activity, and, if the students can handle it, a fairly free discussion should follow, based on one or two questions from the teacher, e.g. 'Do you think they all *really* support the plan? How do you know?'

At a lower level, some practice can be given using more specific questions, e.g. 'Is Peter angry?', or charts to fill in followed by brief discussion of how the students reached their decisions.

In this example, the activity follows a listening text consisting of interviews between David Freeman, a chat-show host, and a group of actors and actresses.

EXAMPLE

3
And what about the interviewer, David Freeman?

a) How does he get his guests to talk?
Does he ask a lot of questions?
Does he talk a lot himself?
Does he talk about himself very much?
In your opinion, does he talk too much?
too little? too quickly?

b) Which of these adjectives would you use to describe him?

amusing	interesting	stimulating
boring	interested in people	vain
bossy	lively	warm
friendly	precise	well informed

From Donn Byrne *The David Freeman Show* Student's Book, page 17. Modern English Publications 1985

7.4.11
Role-
play/simulation

Role-play and simulation are activities which can be based on a number of different stimuli: role cards, stories, characters seen on television, etc, as well as listening passages. The attraction of using listening as an input is that it can provide the students with a selection of language appropriate to the roles and situations which are to be developed. Even if the situation presented in the listening text is different from the one to be used in the role-play, it is useful for the students to hear relevant language functions and forms which they may wish to use when their turn comes to speak.

Since role-play and simulation are less tightly linked to the actual listening than most of the other activities described in this chapter, published listening material does not usually incorporate such activities, but it is often possible to follow the pre- and while-listening activities associated with a text by a role-play/simulation to help the students transfer some of the language learned from listening into their spoken repertoire (as in **5** in the example on the next page).

EXAMPLE

3. Listen in 📼

Some people are shopping for different things in a big department store. Look at the pictures. Then listen to the conversations and match each conversation with its picture.

1 2 3 4
a b c d

5. Your turn
A customer in the department store wants to buy some sunglasses. Act out the conversation between the customer and the clerk. Use this information:

The customer wants to see some brown glasses.
They're next to some red glasses.
The glasses are $15.50 ($16.74 with tax).

Customer: How much are those glasses?
Clerk: These?...

Customer	Clerk
Asks how much the glasses are. ("...those glasses?")	Points to some black glasses. ("These?")
Points out the glasses he wants. ("No, the ones...")	Says how much the glasses are.
Asks to try the glasses on. ("May I try them on?")	Gives the glasses to the customer.
Says he'll take them.	Asks if customer needs anything else.
Doesn't need anything else.	Says how much the glasses are with tax.

4. Say it right 📼

Practice this conversation.

● I like the red sunglasses. How much are they?

○ $14.95. (fourteen ninety-five)

● And the brown ones...how much are they?

○ $12.95. (twelve ninety-five)

87

From Diane Warshawsky with Donald R H Byrd *Spectrum 1*, page 87. Regents, New York, 1982

7.4.12
Dictation

For many people, the word 'dictation' conjures up a picture of a class full of students busily attempting to reproduce, in written form, a piece of prose read aloud by a teacher. In one sense, this could be seen as a while-listening activity, but when dictation is done in this way the aim is usually for the students to produce a correct written version free from spelling errors. If, on the other hand, the aim is to get students to concentrate on the listening text, or parts of it, the emphasis should not be on spelling and writing correct English sentences but on sorting out the meaning of the words spoken. Since naturally spoken language contains many elisions and assimilations, the student often needs to disentangle it in order to produce a written version. The accuracy of the written version (whether the student writes, for example, 'What do you want?' or 'What d'you want?') is not particularly important. What is wanted is that the student's version indicates comprehension of the utterances, and writing them down is one way of showing this comprehension. Teachers sometimes simply ask students to show that they have understood by repeating various bits of the listening text orally, but this is not always a reliable guide, as some students are able to mimic sounds without knowing what they mean.

Whilst gap-filling, using no more than three or four words per gap, is a valid while-listening activity, anything which requires more continuous written reproduction of exact words should be treated separately. A common format in published materials, and one which works well, is that, after the students have heard the listening text and done some while-listening work on it, they are asked to complete the exact words spoken at specific points by going back and listening again.

This can be done satisfactorily with a whole class using one playback machine provided that the part to be written down is relatively short. If longer extracts are to be reproduced in writing, a listening centre or language laboratory where students can control their own machines provides a much more successful situation.

7.5
Post-listening integrated skills work and motivation

In Chapter 5 section 5.9, attention was drawn to the way in which pre-listening work provides opportunities for listening to be integrated with all the other skills in the learning programme. Similar comments can be made about those post-listening activities which naturally lead on from the listening text to other work. Indeed, it is believed by some people that all language learning should *start* from listening comprehension rather than, as is often the case, that listening comprehension should be added on to an established programme of reading, writing and speaking. In reality, the order and organisation of lessons is often not in the hands of individual teachers, nor are they able to choose what material to use. But whatever the circumstances, all teachers have some opportunities, however few, to give their students listening experiences and to integrate these into their total programme.

By using some of the post-listening ideas listed in this chapter, you will be able to make links forward from listening, in much the same way as you can link listening on to other work through pre-listening activities.

The pitfall to avoid in post-listening work is that of boredom for the students. The increasing interest in, and success with, listening work is perhaps in large part due to the 'new' approach to listening. For many years, the routine was listening followed by questions to answer. Now, much listening work follows the pattern of (i) a pre-listening buildup, leading to a desire to listen; (ii) something interesting to listen to and a purpose for listening (generally a while-listening activity); and (iii) a brief (or perhaps no) post-listening stage. It is important to stress that motivation at the post-listening stage is greatly enhanced if the activity has some purpose of its own and is of itself motivating, rather than depending on the intrinsic interest of the text.

Listening should be looked upon not as an appendage, but as an integral part of the total package of learning, sometimes leading to and sometimes emerging from other work.

Discussion

1 Which post-listening activities are particularly relevant for your students? Which ones would you find difficult to handle in your teaching situation?
2 Having read the chapters on pre-, while- and post-listening, do you feel you should change the emphasis you place on one or other of these three stages?

Exercises

1 Consider any set of post-listening comprehension questions. How could you present them differently (whilst still eliciting the same responses) to make them more interesting for your students?
2 Identify two or three listening texts which could give rise to appropriate role-play/simulation for one of your classes. Plan an activity and then try it out.

References

1 Geddes, M and Sturtridge, G 1979 *Listening Links*. Heinemann

PART 3

8

Recorded material or 'live' presentation?

Over recent years recorded material of some kind has generally formed the basis of most listening comprehension work. Whilst there are advantages to using recorded material, there are also good reasons for the teacher fulfilling the role of speaker on some occasions, and even for students, and perhaps visitors, to take a turn at being the speaker. This chapter identifies sources of material and considers the advantages of both recorded and 'live' presentations.

**8.1
Sources of
material**

In addition to the listening exercises which are sometimes found in coursebooks, a range of specially designed listening material is available from publishers. Publications usually consist of audio recordings on cassette, accompanied by books containing activities for students, and, often, a teacher's book.

While the quality and quantity of listening included in a coursebook are unlikely to be the main criteria when deciding which book is best for your students, they are clearly the most important considerations when selecting supplementary listening materials. In Chapter 10, suggestions are made on criteria to apply when choosing recorded material.

As well as using published cassettes/tapes, it is possible in some countries to use radio and television programmes which can be recorded 'off air', although copyright restrictions may limit what may be recorded. If you are allowed to copy 'off air', it is important to ensure that the quality of your recording is good enough for your purposes.

Some ministries of education hold collections of material and, in some parts of the world, material can be borrowed from the British Council. If you plan to use material from such collections as these, you will normally need to make arrangements for borrowing it well in advance. The position varies from country to country, but it is worth exploring the possibilities, particularly if you teach in a place where it is difficult to obtain a range of material and/or where published materials are very expensive to buy and the only books which can be bought by your school are the basic coursebooks.

Even where material is readily available, some teachers like to make their own recordings. If you plan to act as the speaker yourself, there is virtually an endless supply of source material. Every story you know, every book, paper, magazine you have available, every game you can think of, everything you can make or do – all these can form the basis of listening activities. Finding the source material is not a problem at all, but producing appropriate activities to go with it takes time and effort because you have to prepare all the activities which published materials provide as part of the 'package'.

8.2
The advantages of using 'live' presentations

What frequently occurs in classes is that teachers talk to their students and the students listen. Sometimes (less often perhaps), students talk and teachers listen, and sometimes students talk to their fellow students. All of these exchanges contribute to the students' listening experience and teachers should consciously provide as much genuine communicative input as possible. 'What did you say, Ulrich?' 'Can you all see the picture?' 'Guess what happened to me on my way home yesterday' – all of these everyday utterances can provide useful listening practice for the students.

It is, however, usually necessary to supplement this listening with more formal practice, both to widen the students' range of experience and, often, to prepare for examinations.

The main advantage of the teacher, or other 'live' speakers, providing the discourse is that:

(a) the speaker can be seen, and so the listeners have all the non-verbal clues available to help them decipher the message. They see the facial expressions, the gestures, the movement of the head/body.

(b) the listeners' reactions are seen/heard by the speaker. This should (but does not always!) influence both what the speaker says and how he/she says it.

(c) experienced teachers are often particularly skilled at adjusting the level of difficulty as they go along if they see that their listeners are having problems. They can increase the length of pauses, they can repeat bits of what they are saying, they can add explanations, they can use simpler words, and so on.

(d) a speaker present in a room is nearly always easier to hear than a recorded voice (provided that the speaker speaks clearly and loudly enough).

(e) there is no need to organise equipment in advance and there are no problems with machines that do not work properly.

8.3
The advantages of using recorded material

There are, however, advantages in using recorded material. The main ones are that:

(a) a much wider variety of listening experiences can be brought to the students. They might listen to a speech, a news report, a conversation between two or three people. They can hear different speakers, with different accents, speaking at different speeds. The recordings might be enhanced by including appropriate background sounds or music.

(b) in situations where the teacher's mother tongue is not English, it provides opportunities for students to hear native speakers of the language and, sometimes, fluent non-native speakers from other parts of the world.

(c) the recording can be replayed over and over again and will always be the same. In face-to-face conversation, a request for something to be repeated generally leads to a slightly different version of what was said and so the listener does not get a second attempt at understanding precisely what he/she failed to grasp the first time. For example: 'Do you want to come with me?' 'Sorry. What did you say?' 'I asked you if you'd like to come with me.'

For practice purposes, the recording behaves like an infinitely patient speaker who will repeat and repeat without varying the words, intonation or tone. Clearly this aspect should not be overestimated, as part of the skill of listening is concerned with not worrying about parts we have missed. However, there are times when it is possible, and desirable, to replay a recording a number of times (see Chapter 6, 'The while-listening stage').

(d) not being able to see the speaker means that the students must concentrate on what they hear, rather than perhaps guessing the meaning of what is said from the paralinguistic signals (the nods, the smiles, etc). This listening without seeing the speaker prepares students for those situations in everyday life where they must depend solely on the auditory channel for the receipt of information: when they are on the telephone or listening to the radio, for example.

(e) the teacher can prepare the whole listening activity before arriving at the class, either by selecting recorded material or by recording it him/herself. Some teachers might choose to pre-record their own material in this way, so that groups or individual students can use it at different times, perhaps in the listening centre or as an extra activity for those who finish other work faster than their fellow students.

(f) students may be able to work alone and in their own time. This is often the case where a listening centre has been set up or when students are permitted to take cassettes home to listen to.

8.4
The use of video in listening work

The use of video recordings enables teachers to point out the many visual clues which listeners use to help them understand what they hear. Students will see whether the speakers are young or old, happy or angry, requesting or complaining. They will see the physical context in which the speakers are speaking. They will see the facial expressions and gestures and, in some instances, the reactions of those whom the speaker is addressing. Even if the video presents nothing more than a single shot of a solitary speaker (as in the case of a recorded lecture, perhaps), students will still benefit from being able to see the gestures and facial expression and lip movements of the speaker. All of these factors are important not only because they contribute to the immediate act of comprehension, but because they help the students to build up the kind of knowledge of context which is important for successful listening.

For listening practice, video seems to combine most of the advantages of using audio recordings with the main advantage of 'live' presentation, i.e. that the speaker and the immediate context in which he/she is speaking can be seen. But it is significant that the verbs used in relation to television and video are 'to watch' and 'to view'. We rarely refer to anyone 'listening to' television. Often viewers can understand quite a lot of what is being transmitted simply by watching, and do not need to listen particularly carefully. For this reason, when using video for listening work, students should be provided with tasks which necessitate listening as well as watching.

Conclusion

A mixture of 'live' and recorded material will provide the best mix of listening for students, and will bring them the *range* of listening experiences which is so important in developing their skills. Video recordings have an important part to play in listening work, but they should not be used to the exclusion of material spoken by teachers and other speakers, nor recorded material from audio tapes/cassettes.

Discussion

1 What sources of material do you use at present? Why do you use them? Are there any other sources which you might explore?
2 What proportion of the listening work you do with your own students is based on 'live' speakers and how much is based on recorded material? Should you change these proportions in the light of what you have read in this chapter and in Chapters 2 and 3?

Exercises

1 Make a list of the possible sources of material in the area in which you teach. First consider whether there are any as yet 'untapped' sources of recorded material which you might explore. Then list sources of printed material which you could use as the basis of 'live' listening activities.
2 Think of an experience which you have had in the past which you would be happy to tell your students about. Make notes of the main points and then check whether you can retell the story in language which you think your students can handle well enough to be able to follow, without necessarily understanding every word.

9

Authentic or non-authentic material?

One of the well-known surprises of arriving in a foreign country on a first visit is the fact that, in spite of years of language study at school, one is unable to understand what is being said. The lessons learned in the classroom do not seem to have been adequate preparation for the 'real thing'.

It is now generally accepted that students need to practise listening to the kind of speech they will actually encounter in real life so that they will be able to understand and respond to what English speakers are saying.

This chapter draws attention to the features which characterise 'authentic' and 'non-authentic' speech and, whilst recognising that there is reluctance on the part of some teachers to use authentic materials, advocates a move towards materials which present spontaneous, unscripted speech.

9.1
Authentic speech – definitions

Since the early 1970s, there has been much debate about what constitutes authentic speech and about the value of using authentic speech in listening work.

In trying to establish a definition, phrases like 'real speech', 'not specially designed for foreign learners', 'natural conversation', 'what people say in real life', 'what native speakers say when talking to each other' have been used. Many examples of where it might be heard have been given, including 'in the street', 'at home', 'on some radio programmes', 'at meetings', 'in school', etc.

The strictest distinction between 'authentic' and 'non-authentic' is made clear by David Forman (1986),[1] who says:

> Any text is 'authentic' if it was produced in response to real life communicative needs rather than as an imitation of real life communicative needs. The term can be applied to any sort of text, written or spoken, and in relation to any kind of situation of language use. A text purporting to be a radio news bulletin is authentic if it really is a radio news bulletin and is not authentic if it was produced – however

skillfully – for some other purpose, e.g. as an imitation of a radio news bulletin for purposes of language teaching. The script of a play is authentic play script, but not authentic conversation.

9.2 Non-authentic material

When material which was not designed to be spoken (e.g. a novel) is spoken aloud, it obviously lacks the naturalness and spontaneity of ordinary speech. But even material written especially for recording (e.g. dialogue scripts) fails to match the kind of speech produced naturally by people who are simply talking to each other. This lack of naturalness and spontaneity occurs to varying degrees. A well-written dialogue spoken by good actors and actresses can get very near to sounding authentic, whilst a hastily written dialogue recorded by two or three teachers may sound exceedingly non-authentic as they perhaps, often unconsciously, speak more clearly and more slowly than the average person would in a normal conversation.

A fair amount of the material being used for listening practice and for listening tests falls into the non-authentic category. It usually consists of prose read aloud or recordings of scripted conversations. But many teachers and some examination boards have now turned to material which provides something much more like authentic speech, even if it is not truly authentic.

9.3 Features of non-authentic speech

There are a number of features which distinguish non-authentic speech from authentic speech. Each one of these features may or may not exist, or may exist to a greater or lesser degree, in any particular piece of spoken discourse.
Non-authentic speech might exhibit:

– unnatural rhythm;
– unnatural intonation;
– over-clear enunciation;
– little overlap between speakers;
– slow (and perhaps monotonous) delivery;
– structured language which was meant to be read silently rather than spoken aloud;
– complete sentences as utterances;
– no background noise;
– artificial stops and starts;
– densely packed information.

9.4 Problems with non-authentic materials

Students working with non-authentic materials are led into false expectations about what will occur in the ordinary spoken language which they will wish to understand. By using clearly non-authentic texts for listening, we can cause students the additional problem of having to try to transfer what they have learned by listening to non-authentic materials to their attempts to understand authentic speech. For this reason, there is now considerable support for using authentic material or 'near authentic' material (i.e. really good imitations, which incorporate the features of authentic speech) from the earliest stages as a significant part of the students' listening experience.

9.5
Features of
authentic speech

The features which characterise authentic speech are the converse of those listed in 9.3. In other words, authentic speech will probably have:

– natural rhythm;
– natural intonation;
– natural pronunciation (i.e. not especially carefully enunciated);
– some overlap between speakers (including interruptions);
– normal rate of delivery (sometimes fast, sometimes slow);
– relatively unstructured language, which is used spontaneously in speech;
– incomplete sentences, false starts, hesitations;
– background noises and, sometimes, background voices;
– natural starts and stops;
– less densely packed information than in written language.

9.6
Merits of
authentic speech

Authentic material allows the students to hear a much more real act of communication with all the interactional features which are normally not found in scripted materials. It gives them a true representation of real, spontaneous speech with its hesitations, false starts and 'mistakes', which will make them more able to cope with 'real life' speech when they meet it outside the learning situation.

If students have the opportunity to listen to a range of authentic texts, they will sample many different voices, with varying accents, both social and regional. They will hear people expressing things in a variety of ways; for example, they may hear anger being expressed by shouting or by choice of words or by many interruptions.

9.7
The crucial factor

Over the years, writers and teachers have spent long hours considering the exact meaning and relative merits of using speech which is 'authentic', 'authentic-sounding', 'non-authentic', 'semi-scripted', 'semi-authentic', and so on. Fortunately, we have now come to realise that the exact definition of all these terms is not really crucial for our purposes. What *is* crucial is that students should listen to ordinary speech, spoken by ordinary people in their ordinary ways. It may or may not be truly 'authentic' speech, but, provided that it is realistic (i.e. like real life, with the characteristics of unrehearsed speech), it will give students the kind of practice they need.

9.8
Reluctance to
use authentic
material

The main reason teachers give for not using authentic materials is that such materials are too difficult. True, authentic materials cannot be graded before they are produced (though some grading can be achieved by careful selection of pieces after recording, using criteria such as number of speakers, accents, topic, etc), and so teachers are unlikely to find *precisely* the right texts to match their coursebooks. They may find texts with suitable language, but spoken in a way which is difficult to follow, or they may have tapes on which the delivery is good, but the language is far too difficult.

If authentic and near-authentic texts are to be used from the earliest stages, then it is important to use them for limited purposes, with aims which the students can achieve. For example, you could ask the students to decide, in general, what the situation is, what kind of person is speaking and to whom (a boss?/a child?/a teenager to a friend?) and what they are discussing.

What students are asked to *do* is as important as the simplicity or otherwise of the listening text itself. Relatively difficult texts can be used if the listeners are well prepared and if they are asked to carry out only very simple tasks, which do not depend on total comprehension of the whole text.

A listening text should not be judged to be too difficult merely because the students will not be able to understand every word and follow every bit of what is said. This is not the way native speakers approach listening in their own language, and students should be taught not to expect it to happen when they listen to English.

Another reason why teachers show reluctance to use authentic material is that they sometimes fail to distinguish between 'authentic' and 'recorded' when discussing material, and tend to associate all they dislike about poor recordings with authentic material, or they confuse authentic with informal chat, which is indeed sometimes difficult to use.

It is important to remember that the most authentic speech is provided by the teacher going about the daily tasks of running the class (if, that is, the teacher is not 'filtering' or adjusting the language level to the level of the class too much), and so this should not be undervalued as a contribution to the development of the students' listening skills.

Conclusion

In this chapter, we have looked at the features of both non-authentic and authentic speech. We have recognised that authentic or near-authentic material can be used even with early learners, provided that the associated tasks are easy enough to be carried out successfully.

Students need to experience as wide a selection of listening texts as possible. Whether these texts are always authentic is not such an important issue. What *is* important is that listening work should not be limited to prose read aloud and coursebook tapes, and that a range of listening experiences should be introduced based on speech which is as near to authentic as possible. Teachers should not wait until their students have become advanced learners to begin using authentic materials, although at first texts will have to be selected carefully and tasks kept simple, so that students are not demotivated by being confronted with texts and activities which they cannot handle.

Discussion

1 What authentic materials do you think it is possible to use with a beginners' group? How would you use them?
2 What do you see as the main advantage of using authentic materials?

Exercises

1 Listen to one or two listening texts from material available to you and try to decide how they were recorded. Are they authentic, semi-scripted (i.e. spoken from notes), or scripted (read from a text)? How do you know?
2 Prepare notes for a semi-scripted recording session for two speakers. Use these notes to make a recording.

References

1 Forman, D 1986 *Factors affecting the choice of relevant listening material for Malaysian students planning to study at English medium institutes of higher education overseas.* University of Wales Institute of Science and Technology, Cardiff (unpublished)

10

Criteria for the selection of recorded material

10.1
Why criteria are useful

Most teachers simply do not have the time, or the opportunity, or perhaps even the interest, to record their own listening material for their classes. The technical problems of making good quality recordings, even from radio, let alone the difficulties of collecting authentic speech, make it uneconomical for many teachers to do it for themselves. It is important to have criteria against which to measure any recorded texts which can be obtained, so that decisions can be made about whether any particular part is suitable for a certain group of students.

Sometimes the choice of texts is limited, but the criteria will also assist you in deciding what steps you should take to compensate for any deficiencies you find in a listening text.

Before using a listening text in class, you will want to know something about its language, its length, its content, the style and speed of the delivery, how close to 'real' speech it is and the quality of the recording.

10.2
The criteria
10.2.1
Language

Using listening texts of the right level (combined with appropriate activities) will not only develop listening skills but will also contribute to students' overall language learning. Stephen Krashen has identified listening as a valuable source of what he calls 'comprehensible input'.[1] Krashen maintains that students need both to *acquire* a language and to *learn* a language. For Krashen, *learning* is a conscious process of studying and understanding bits of the language step by step, while *acquisition* is a subconscious process which occurs naturally under certain conditions. Being exposed to 'comprehensible input' contributes, in Krashen's view, to this process. By 'comprehensible input', Krashen means a flow of language which contains elements already known plus some which have yet to be mastered. Students should be faced with language which they should be capable of understanding although it is slightly above their current level of use.

It is not possible, nor even desirable, to 'match' listening material, especially authentic material, exactly with the language being taught at any particular time. However, you will want to select listening texts which provide 'comprehensible input' and which are at approximately the right level of difficulty. It is important to 'stretch' students in this way as it seems that, with practice, comprehension develops more rapidly than speaking or writing skills, and most students respond well to the challenge.

10.2.2
Length

There is no doubt that it is difficult for most elementary and intermediate level students to listen attentively (not just to hear) for anything more than about two minutes without a break of some sort. As we noted in Chapter 3, section 3.1, many students struggle to grasp every word and this makes the task even harder. Of course it is easier to pay attention for longer if the subject matter of the listening text is particularly interesting, or if the listeners have a specific task to do in relation to the text.

On the other hand, very short passages of, say, half a minute or less sometimes cause problems because the students do not have time to get used to the voice(s) or to tune in to the topic, and the whole thing is over before they get to grips with it. For this reason, it is most important that students should be given more pre-listening preparation when short texts are being used, so that they know what to expect when the tape is played and can, therefore, tune in more rapidly.

There can be no hard and fast rule about the length of a listening text for a particular level. If you have a text which you want to use but find rather long, you should plan to stop the tape from time to time, and use it in more manageable sections and introduce pauses (or extra pauses) to give your students time to think.

If you are using published material with the students' work printed in a workbook, you will need to check that your stops fit in with the work to be done. Many books indicate where it is appropriate and convenient to stop the tape and you have only to ensure that you understand the symbols in the book and can operate the 'pause' and 'stop' buttons on the cassette recorder efficiently. In the following example of a published transcript, a single line (/) indicates a pause on the actual recording, and a double line (//) is used to indicate a place where the teacher is advised to stop the machine.

TRANSCRIPT

To complete the magic number square, you must first, put the number 2 in the top left corner./ Then, put the number 6 in the top right corner./ Write a 4 in the bottom left corner/ and an 8 in the bottom right corner./

Now you must put a number in the middle square on each side, so that the numbers along each side add up to 15.//

Finally, put a number in the middle square, so that each row and each column, and each of the diagonals add up to 15.//

Do you notice anything interesting about the numbers?//

From Mary Underwood *Better Listening 1* Teacher's Book, page 13. Oxford University Press, Hong Kong, 1986

**10.2.3
Content**

In the early stages, students have to cope with a lot of problems while they are listening. They do not know what sounds will occur, how fast the language is to be spoken, what the intonation signifies, what pauses are used for, or even whether the speaker is angry or pleased, asking or telling. It is, therefore, important at this stage to use plain, straightforward content so that the number and variety of their problems is reduced. For example, texts should be avoided if they jump backwards and forwards in time, or deal with very abstract concepts, or are full of jargon words (unless particularly relevant to an ESP – English for Special Purposes – group), or are not logically sequenced, etc.

Care should be taken, however, not to treat students as less mature intellectually because they lack mastery of the language. Fortunately, the time has passed when adult learners of foreign languages were expected to use the same textbooks as young children and were expected to follow childish stories and make childish utterances.

All students need material which will involve them and make them want to listen. The difficulty for teachers lies in identifying appropriate material which *does* interest people. One cannot simply provide teenagers, for example, with endless pop songs and ask them to endeavour to write down the words. This is a popular activity and one which many students enjoy, but it only exposes them to a very narrow selection of language (some of which is very esoteric!). On the other hand, they will not respond well to a week-by-week diet of dull, predictable material consisting of readings from their coursebook followed by questions.

Texts which deal with up-to-the-minute news and the very latest ideas are often of considerable interest, but they soon get out of date and are of no interest to students attending the course the following year. Teachers who invest a lot of time preparing activities for their classes need to judge how much material of this kind they can 'afford' to use. If the same material is to be used in ensuing years, topics which are less ephemeral must be sought.

Funny stories and amusing pictures can be exploited to great effect in language teaching, but they should not be the sole type of material used. Fortunately, textbook writers now seem to agree with this view, and, whilst not abandoning the idea that students should enjoy their classes, incorporate a wider and more thought-provoking range of topics and style.

It is true that funny stories may hold attention, but so do a lot of other stories. The 'fun' is often greater when those carrying out the listening work are enjoying what they are doing, rather than doing dull work based on a funny text. Also, much that is serious is of interest, even to young students. You need to discover what topics your students find interesting and then to provide them with a wide range of stimulating material, choosing texts which lend themselves to pre-listening work of the kinds described in Chapter 5.

**10.2.4
The use of visual
support material**

Visual material can be helpful to students, especially if the topic is not related to something from their everyday lives. A relevant picture will focus attention on the topic, and one can also use maps, charts, models, etc. It may be possible to find a large enough picture or chart to hang on the wall for all the class to see. It is sometimes a good idea to hang the picture up in advance so that the students have an opportunity to get close to it and have a really careful look; then when the picture is used in the lesson, they may already have thought about it and will be better able to respond to questions or comments.

A large picture, well displayed, can be used in pre-listening work in a variety of ways. But if the students are going to *use* the picture in carrying out activities, they will generally need to have a copy each.

It is often through pictures and other illustrative material that listening work can be integrated with reading, writing and speaking skills. For this reason, you may decide to look for potentially interesting visual material and then develop a range of activities, including listening activities, based upon it. Or you may prefer one text to another from the material available simply because you can find good visual material to accompany it, and you can then devise reading, writing or speaking activities to produce integrated skills work. And, of course, you may choose a particular video recording for listening work because the pictures are especially appropriate for the particular purpose.

In Chapters 5, 6 and 7 there are lots of examples of the use of visual materials in listening work.

10.2.5 The style of delivery	Every individual has his/her own way of speaking – some people speak quickly, others slowly; some give more stress to significant words than others do; some vary their pitch or their volume more than others. It is easier for students if, at least in the early stages of their learning, they are not faced with too many variables at once. For this reason, they should at first be presented with listening texts which are spoken without excessive or sudden changes in speed or pitch or volume. This does not mean that a text spoken slowly and in a flat tone should be used. Indeed, such a text, as well as giving a completely wrong impression of how the language is spoken, would be very boring and demotivating. A 'good' text at this stage is one spoken by a person whose natural speed of speech is quite slow and deliberate, but who has a pleasant tone and varied pitch (but see 10.2.6 below).

Also, at this early stage, students may have difficulty in differentiating between voices, and so there should generally be no more than two, or possibly three, speakers to recognise. Even with only two voices, it is sometimes difficult to tell who is speaking. Most producers of published material, however, do go to some trouble to use voices which contrast well.

Clearly, unless the students are living in, or destined for, a specific region, the speakers on the recording should not have very strong regional accents. Nevertheless, it is unrealistic to go to the other extreme and use only recordings made by RP (received pronunciation) speakers or Midwest Standard US speakers. It is not necessary to wait for students to become very proficient before introducing them to gentle accents and varieties of speech, although they will not be expected to imitate these accents or varieties, nor to incorporate them into their own repertoire of spoken English. They should, however, learn to understand a variety of voices sufficiently well to be able to communicate with a wide range of people.

The transition to material which incorporates a wider variety of styles and voices should be done gradually. The speed of this transition must be determined by the progress made by the students, who should not be pressed too hard, since confidence, which is an essential prerequisite for success in listening, can all too easily be destroyed by one or two unsuccessful experiences.

10.2.6
The speed of delivery

The words of a text should be spoken at normal speed, not slowed down in an attempt to help the students.

Some people speak more slowly than others naturally and it is an advantage to have such speakers to listen to in the early stages. A person whose natural speech is fast but who slows down for the sake of the foreign listener is usually not a good model. Speech which is deliberately slowed down loses a great deal of its natural rhythm and intonation, and this confuses rather than helps the listener.

Far more important than the speed of uttering the words is the length of the pauses between groups of words. These pauses give the listener time to sort out the part of the message just received and provide time for him/her to prepare to receive the next part.

It is sometimes possible for the teacher to lengthen the pauses in commercially produced material as it is being used in class, by pressing the pause button on the tape/cassette recorder to stop the tape for a second or two. This, however, needs advance preparation (and practice at first) as you need to know precisely where you intend to stop the tape. It is easiest to do it by marking your transcript and then following the script carefully when you are playing the tape in the class, so that you do not make mistakes and cause more problems for your students.

This method works in the language laboratory or listening laboratory too, as the master tape can be stopped while the students' machines, onto which the material is being copied, are allowed to run on, so that the students' cassettes include longer 'silences' than were incorporated in the original recording. In this situation, the students are all left with a copy of the tape which includes the enhanced pauses, which means that they can listen to the text in exactly the same form over and over again.

To use this same method to make just a single copy in preparation for a lesson, you will need two cassette recorders and a suitable lead to link them together. You then make a copy of the recording, stopping the master tape for a couple of seconds at the pauses you have marked on your transcript and letting the copy tape run on. The copy can then be used, with its longer pauses, in the classroom, thus enabling you to avoid the difficulties associated with lengthening the pauses there and then. Another advantage of this method is that the job of lengthening the pauses can be done just once and the copy kept for further use.

Sometimes, teachers are tempted to use the transcript of a recording as a script from which to rerecord the whole thing themselves, or using actors or other speakers, in order to produce a slower version of the original, or even just to lengthen the pauses. This is *not* a good idea. So much is lost in 'naturalness' that it usually creates more problems than it solves.

10.2.7
Spontaneity

The importance of providing listening material which presents the features of spontaneous speech was emphasised in Chapter 2. This means choosing texts which are as 'real' as possible rather than ones which have been specially scripted or prepared to demonstrate particular language forms or functions.

Inevitably, spontaneous speech will include repetitions, false starts and hesitations, which students need to get used to hearing and dealing with. For example, they need to learn the skill of letting unimportant sections of what is heard pass, as it were, 'unattended' while they focus on those parts which convey vital information.

Spontaneous speech will also include some 'redundant' parts (parts which contribute little to the essential message). These provide processing time in much the same way that pauses do and are a valuable feature for the listener. It is, therefore, very important for a listening text not to be stripped of its 'redundant' parts, because the listener cannot process such language, even in his/her own language, fast enough to cope with all it contains.

10.2.8
The quality of production

There is little point in playing tapes to students if they cannot hear them clearly. Commercially produced recordings are generally of acceptable quality in this regard, but care should be taken to check that a recording which is quite clear to one listener sitting beside the tape/cassette player will also be clearly audible to a whole group in the classroom or wherever else the group will be working.

Part of the problem of not being able to hear a recording clearly is often to be found in the learning situation itself, rather than in the level and quality of the recording. Such things as poor acoustics in the teaching room, noises from adjacent rooms or from outside, poor quality equipment, all create difficulties for listening work. Recognising that these difficulties exist, it is all the more important to check that the recorded material itself is of the highest possible quality.

On some recordings there are sounds that can be heard in the background – other voices, or music, or the noise of traffic or machines, etc. It may be tempting to reject recordings which have such noise on them, again in an attempt to reduce the students' problems. But background sounds which give an indication of the context are often helpful to the listener and, of course, provide a much more realistic listening situation. The recording to be avoided is the one where the background is distracting, or so loud as to be confused with the voice(s) to be listened to, or simply so disagreeable as to put the listener off.

A carefully produced tape, which has none of the irritations of a badly produced tape (clunks and clicks, changing levels, etc) is generally easier to listen to. And a tape which has something 'extra' – a bit of music, perhaps, or good sound effects, or a friendly presenter – can make listening more pleasant.

Conclusion

In this chapter, we have looked at some criteria against which we might judge how appropriate a particular recorded text is for a specific group of students. We have noted the importance of finding well-recorded material of the right length, with interesting content, delivered in a comprehensible style and at a suitable speed.

Discussion

1 Which two of the criteria mentioned in this chapter do you think are the most important?

2 Are there any other criteria which you would add?

Exercises

1 Concentrating on one group of students you teach, make a list of topics which they would find interesting. Then look through any published material you have available and check whether any of these topics occur.

2 Check one listening text against the suggested criteria and decide whether you would want to use it. Use the chart on the next page for this exercise. Then decide what use, if any, the chart might be to you in the future.

The example given in the first column of the chart is a check done on an activity from *Better Listening 1* by Mary Underwood (Oxford University Press, Hong Kong, 1986). The material is intended for eleven to twelve year olds in Hong Kong secondary schools. The Student's Book shows the activity like this:

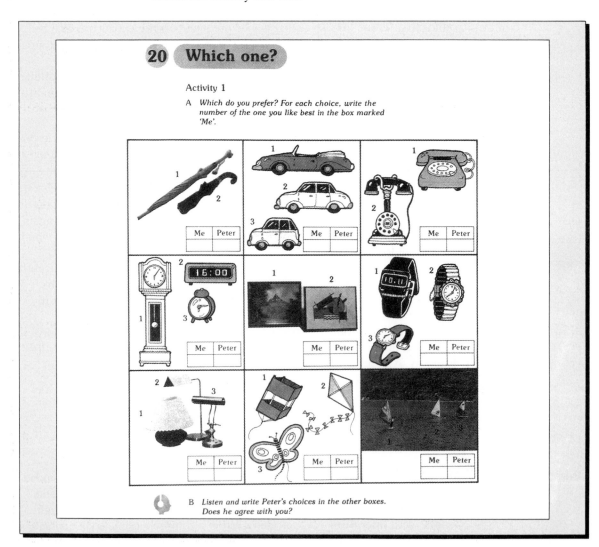

The Teacher's Book contains teaching notes and the transcript:

JANE: Which umbrella do you prefer, Peter?

PETER: I prefer the long one, with the straight handle./

JANE: And the cars? Which one do you prefer?

PETER: Oh, that's easy. I like the long, low sports car./

JANE: I thought you'd choose that one! What about the phones? Do you prefer the modern one or the old-fashioned one?

PETER: I think I prefer the old-fashioned one./

JANE: What about the lamps?

PETER: I prefer the tall, simple one. I like a lamp that's useful, not just made to look pretty./

JANE: Do you like simple pictures, too? What about the pictures?

PETER: I don't like modern art much. I'd choose the country scene, with all those lovely trees and fields./

JANE: What about the clocks? Which clock do you prefer?

PETER: Oh, I love the big, old grandfather clock. My grandparents have got one and I think it's beautiful./

JANE: What about watches? Do you like big watches?

PETER: I've just got a new watch. And I chose a digital one. So I suppose I prefer digital ones, at present. Of those three, I prefer the black one, with the black strap./

JANE: What about kites? Have you got a kite?

PETER: Oh, yes. I've got a kite, just an ordinary one. But I prefer box-kites, so I'd choose the, um, the red box-kite, I think./

JANE: Do you like wind-surfing? Which sail do you like best?

PETER: I'm not very keen on wind-surfing, but I think I like the white sail best. The one in the middle./ What about you, Jane? Which sail do you like?

JANE: I don't like any of them. I'm not keen on wind-surfing either.//

CRITERIA FOR THE SELECTION OF RECORDED MATERIAL

FOR CLASS _____	TITLE AND REFERENCE OF TEXT		
	"Which One?" Better Listening Book 1 Unit 20 Activity 1		
LANGUAGE	*Function: expressing preference (like, etc)*		
LENGTH	*c 1½ mins*		
CONTENT	*familiar objects · no difficult vocab*		
VISUAL BACKUP	*pictures in work book*		
STYLE OF DELIVERY	*a bit formal, but OK*		
SPEED OF DELIVERY	*fine*		
REDUNDANCY	*some, acceptable*		
QUALITY OF PRODUCTION	*OK*		
SUITABILITY	*best to use after teaching structures*		

References

1 Krashen, S 1977 The Monitor Model for Adult Second Language Performance. In *Viewpoints on English as a Second Language*, Burt, M, Dulay, H and Finocchiaro, M (eds). Regents,

How to succeed with listening work

It is important that students should not be daunted or discouraged by the difficulties they, and sometimes their teachers, perceive in learning to listen to English. Whilst motivation is important in all language learning, it is doubly important in learning to listen, and needs to be coupled with a high level of success from the very beginning.

To help your students develop their confidence and skills, you are urged, when doing listening work:

- to make sure that, before they begin to listen to the speakers (whether on tape or 'live'), the students understand very clearly what they are expected to do, so that they can carry out the planned activities confident that they are doing the right thing;

- to make sure that each time a listening text is heard, even for the second or third or fourth time, the students have a specific purpose for listening;

- to do plenty of pre-listening work, of an appropriate kind for your students, so that they will succeed with whatever listening tasks they are asked to do;

- to encourage all attempts at carrying out the listening tasks, without putting too much emphasis on the quality of the presentation of the response. For example, full sentence responses should not be sought when short ones (even one word) would suffice, as this can slow down the listening work and may well demotivate the students;

- to encourage your students not to worry if they don't understand every word (by, for example, avoiding the temptation to ask them to list the words they do not know, or to learn the new words), as it is very important that they learn to accept that a listening task can often be completed even when they miss some of the words and thus begin to appreciate that comprehension can occur with less than complete understanding of all that is said;

- never to use a recorded listening text in class without having listened to it, not just looked through the transcript, in advance;

- never to take a chance on whether you will be able to operate the particular cassette recorder, or any other piece of equipment, when you arrive in the classroom. Listening work can be totally ruined by incompetent handling of equipment.

Above all, you are urged to treat the listening session as an opportunity for you and your students to enjoy *doing things* in English. Your enthusiasm will certainly enhance their motivation, increase their confidence and help them become successful listeners.

Typology
Pre-listening activities

	Page
— looking at pictures and talking about them	35
— looking at a list of items/thoughts/etc	36
— making lists of possibilities/ideas/suggestions/etc	37
— reading a text	37
— reading through questions (to be answered while listening)	39
— labelling	40
— completing part of a chart	40
— predicting/speculating	42
— pre-viewing language	42
— informal teacher talk and class discussion	43

Typology
While-listening activities

	Page
— marking/checking items in pictures	49
— matching pictures with what is heard	51
— storyline picture sets	52
— putting pictures in order	53
— completing pictures	54
— picture drawing	55
— carrying out actions	55
— making models/arranging items in patterns	56
— following a route	57
— completing grids	58
— form/chart completion	58
— labelling	60
— using lists	62
— true/false	63
— multiple-choice questions	64
— text completion (gap-filling)	65
— spotting mistakes	68
— predicting	69
— seeking specific items of information	72

Typology
Post-listening activities

	Page
— form/chart completion	81
— extending lists	82
— sequencing/'grading'	82
— matching with a reading text	82
— extending notes into written responses	84
— summarising	85
— using information for problem-solving and decision-making activities	86
— jigsaw listening	87
— identifying relationships between speakers	88
— establishing the mood/attitude/behaviour of the speaker	89
— role-play/simulation	90
— dictation	92

Bibliography

Anderson, A and Lynch, T 1988 *Listening*. Oxford University Press

Brazil, D, Coulthard, M and Johns, C 1980 *Discourse Intonation and Language Teaching*. Longman

Brown, G and Yule, G 1983 *Teaching the Spoken Language*. Cambridge University Press

Coulthard, M 1985 *An Introduction to Discourse Analysis*. Longman

ELT Documents Special 1981 *The Teaching of Listening Comprehension*. The British Council

Forman, D 1986 *Factors affecting the choice of relevant listening material for Malaysian students planning to study at English medium institutes of higher education overseas*. Unpublished M Ed thesis, University of Wales Institute of Science and Technology, Cardiff

Galvin, K 1985 *Listening by doing – Developing effective listening skills*. National Textbook Co, Lincoln Wood, Illinois

Garrod, S 1986 Language comprehension in context: a psychological perspective. *Applied Linguistics* **7**(3)

Krashen, S 1981 *Second language acquisition and second language learning*. Pergamon

Mendelsohn, D 1984 There *are* strategies for listening. *TEAL Occasional Papers* **8**

Richards, J 1983 Listening comprehension: approach, design, procedure. *TESOL Quarterly* **1**/(2)

Rixon, S 1986 *Developing Listening Skills*. Macmillan

Stern, H H 1975 What can we learn from the good language learner? *Canadian modern languages review* **31**

Ur, P 1984 *Teaching Listening Comprehension*. Cambridge University Press

Widdowson, H G 1978 *Teaching Language as Communication*. Oxford University Press

Index

Accents 105
Adjusting level of difficulty 25, 34, 46–48, 100–101
Aural reception 2
— echoic memory 2
— long-term memory 2
— processing 2
— short-term memory 2
Authentic activities 31–32
Authentic material 79, 98–101
— grading 100–101 *see also* Adjusting level of difficulty
— reluctance to use 100
Authentic speech 98–99
— definitions 98–99
— features 100
— merits 100

Background knowledge 3

Choosing post-listening activities 80
Choosing pre-listening activities 33–34
Choosing while-listening activities 49
'Comprehensible input' 102–103
Concentration 19
Context 2–4, 9
— 'co-text' 3
— cultural context 22
Conversation 5, 23
Course elements 22

Dictionaries 27

'Eavesdropping' 5, 32
Encouragement 26
Equipment 24

Features of spoken English 9–15
— formal/informal language 14
— organisation of speech 11–12
— pauses and 'fillers' 13–14
— sounds 9–10 *see also* Sounds
— stress and intonation 10–11
— syntax and vocabulary 12–13
Feedback 23, 28, 73
Formal/informal language 14
— organisation 14
— spontaneous speech 14, 106–107
— structured language 14
— 'switches' 14

Grading *see* Adjusting level of difficulty
Groupwork 27

Hearing vs listening 2, 4

Importance of listening 1
Instructions 32–33
— breaking activities into stages 32
— giving a reason for listening 32–33
— need for clarity 32
Integrating listening work 44, 92–93
Intonation and stress 10–11

'Language usage' 4
'Language use' 4
Learning habits 19, 22
Listeners' expectations 30–31
— matching 30
— relationships 30
— topic 30
Listening situations 5–7
— announcements 5
— conversations 5
— 'eavesdropping' 5
— entertainment on TV/radio 6
— instructions 7
— lectures 6
— lessons 6
— 'live' theatre 6
— news/weather forecasts/etc 5
— public address 7
— recordings of songs/etc 6
— telephone 7
— when watching films 5
— when watching TV 5
'Live' presentation 94–97
— advantages 95

Meaning 1, 4, 10, 13, 46, 79
— skill of 'keeping up' 17–18
— 'tolerable'/total comprehension 18
— surface meaning vs interpretation 18, 46
— partial interpretation 22
Mother-tongue listening 1, 96
Motivation 26, 28, 48–49, 78–79, 92–92

'Non-authentic' material 98–101
— definitions 99

— problems 99
'Non-authentic' speech 99
— features 99

'Off-air' recording 94
Organisation of speech 11–12
— change of tone 12
— change of topic 12
— contradictions 12
— disorganised speech 12
— hand/head movements 12
— hesitations 12
— important words 11
— pauses 12 *see also* Pauses in speech
— repetition 11 *see also* Repetition

Pairwork 27, 79
Pauses in speech 12, 13–14
— 'fillers' 13–14
Pausing a recording 103, 106
Planning listening work 23–28
— general considerations 23–25
    control of equipment 24
    location 23
    preparing recordings 24
    selection of equipment 24
    separate lesson/part of lesson 23
    tests 24–25
    time allocation 24
— before the lesson 25–26
    adjusting level 25
    checking activities 25
    choosing text 25
    planning the procedure 26
    practising reading 26
    special equipment 26
    time needed 25
    visual aids 25, 104–105
— during the lesson 26–28
    feedback 28
    giving encouragement 26
    giving help 26
    omitting activities 28
    pair/groupwork 27
    use of dictionaries 27
— conduct of a lesson 28
    pre-, while- and post-listening 28 *see also* Pre-listening, While-listening and Post-listening

Post-listening activities 92
— decision-making 86
— dictation 92
— establishing attitude/mood 89
— identifying relationships 88
— 'jigsaw' listening 87–88
— matching 82–83
— problem-solving 86
— role-play/simulation 90–91
— sequencing/grading 82
— using charts/forms 81–82
— using lists 82
— written work 84–85
Post-listening stage, general
  considerations 74–80
— choosing activities, factors to
  consider 80
— integration 92–93
— methodology 74–77
— motivation 92–93
— nature of activities 78–80
        decision-making/problem-
        solving 78–79
        interpreting 80
        motivation 79–80
        role-play 80
        written work 80
— purpose of activities 74–77
        clarification 75
        discussion of speakers'
        attitudes/manner 77
        discussion of
        content/language 75–77
        expansion 77
        practice for examinations 74
        transfer 77
Prediction 3
Pre-listening activities 34–43
— informal talk 43
— predicting/speculating 42
— previewing language 42–43
— reading 37–39
— using charts 40–41
— using/making lists 36–37
— using pictures 35, 40
Pre-listening stage, general
  considerations 30–44
— adjusting level of difficulty 34
— authentic activities 31–32
— choosing activities, factors to
  consider 33–34
— clear instructions 32

— integration 43–44
— listeners' expectations 30–31
— types of activity 31

Reasons for listening 4–5
Recorded material 94–97
— advantages 95–96
'Redundancy' 107
Repetition 11, 17, 96

Selection of recorded material,
  criteria 102–109
— content 104
— language 102–103
        'comprehensible input'
        102–103
— length 103
— quality of production 107
— speed of delivery 106
        pausing 106
— spontaneity 106–107
        'redundancy' 107
— style of delivery 105–106
        accent 105
        pitch 105
        volume 105
— visual support 104–105 see also
        Visual clues
'Signals' in speech 18, 22–23
Sounds 9–10, 45–46
— distortion 10
— elision 10
— enunciation 10
— in continuous speech 10
— minimal pairs 9–10
— pronunciation 10
Sources of material 94–95
Speed of speech 16, 106
Stress and intonation 10–11
— isolated words vs continuous
  speech 11
— pauses 11, 13–14
— rhythm 10
— stressed syllables 10–11
Syntax and vocabulary 12–13
— incomplete sentences 12–13
— meaning vs structure 13
— non-specific vocabulary 13
— pauses 13
— silences 13

— subordinate clauses 12–13
— use of 'well'/'oh'/etc 13

Teacher's objectives 21–22
— building confidence 22
— exposure 21
— guidance on approaches 21–22
— realistic tasks 21
Teacher's role 21–29, 74–77
Teacher talk 73, 94–96, 101
Types of pre-listening activity 31
— activating prior knowledge 31
— contextualising 31
— narrowing down expectations 31

Video in listening work 96–97
Visual clues 95, 96, 104–105
— Vocabulary 13, 17
        unknown words 17

While-listening activities 49–72
— carrying out actions 55
— following a route 57
— gap-filling 65–67
— information gathering 72
— labelling 60–61
— making models/patterns/etc 56
— multiple-choice questions 64
— predicting 69–71
— spotting mistakes 68
— text completion 65–67
— true/false questions 63
— using charts/grids 58–60
— using lists 62
— using pictures 49–55
While-listening stage, general
  considerations 45–73
— choosing activities, factors to
  consider 49
— feedback 73
— how the language sounds 45
— interpretation 46
— matching 46
— nature of activities 46–49
        interest 46
        level of difficulty 46–48
        motivation 48–49
— prediction at micro/macro levels
  46
— purpose of activities 45–46
— teacher talk 73 see also Teacher
  talk